100 TIPS FOR LADY GOLFERS

It was not until she was seventeen that Kitrina Douglas first held a golf club. Even then, hitting a few shots to amuse herself while her father received a lesson, her natural talent was obvious and was spotted by ex-Scottish international Gordon Cosh.

Within five years she was playing off a plus 2 handicap and had won numerous competitions, including the most prestigious event in amateur golf, The Ladies British Amateur Championship. She represented England five times and Great Britain twice.

At the age of twenty-three, she turned professional and won the first event she entered, the Ford Ladies' Classic at Woburn, finishing the year as Europe's number two lady golfer. Since then she has won nine events on the women's European tour, including the 1989 and 1992 European Masters and 1991 English Open. She was a member of the first European team to defeat the USA in the Solheim Cup.

Kitrina Douglas lives in Bristol.

100 TIPS
for
LADY GOLFERS

KITRINA DOUGLAS

With a Foreword by
Mickey Walker

HarperCollins*Publishers*

For my sisters,
Karen and Kandis

HarperCollins*Publishers*
77–85 Fulham Palace Road, London W6 8JB

First published in Great Britain
in 1993 by HarperCollins*Publishers*

1 3 5 7 9 10 8 6 4 2

Copyright © 1993 Kitrina Douglas

Kitrina Douglas asserts the moral right to be
identified as the author of this work

A catalogue record for this book is
available from the British Library

ISBN 0-551-02737-1

Typeset by Rowland Phototypesetting Limited
Bury St Edmunds, Suffolk
Printed and bound in Great Britain by
Bath Press Colour Books, Glasgow

Contents

PART TWO

CHAPTER 5 TIPS FROM THE GIRLS

CHAPTER 6 EXERCISES FOR GOLF

CHAPTER 7 PRACTICE

PART THREE

CHAPTER 8 PUTTING

ACKNOWLEDGEMENTS

'No Man is an Island'

Throughout my career I have been aided by many people, who have played their part silently in my achievements. When I first started playing golf at Long Ashton there were the ladies who helped me get my first handicap, right from then until now, whilst writing this book, family, friends, teachers and team mates have all played their part in my success.

I would like to thank them all, for the help in the past, present and hopefully the future. My success isn't just down to me.

Lastly and most importantly I would like to thank God for the numerous blessings I have been given and for the ability to play golf.

Foreword

I first met Kitrina in 1984 shortly after she turned professional. She created an immediate impact in professional golf, winning her first event, the Ford Ladies' Classic, at Woburn, and went on to finish second in the order of merit that year.

Since 1984 Kitrina has won eight tournaments, including the 1987 Hennessy Cognac Ladies' Cup, and in 1989 and 1992 the prestigious European Masters. During nine years on the WPG European Tour Kitrina has only twice finished outside the top ten moneywinners, and in 1992 her oustanding play earned her one of the five automatic places in the European Solheim Cup team.

Kitrina's consistently high finishes in tournaments are largely due to the long hours she spends on the practice ground in her search for excellence and knowledge of the golf swing. The articulate and amusing way in which she communicates this knowledge ensures that she is in great demand to give clinics whenever her schedule permits, and on the occasions that we have performed clinics together I have come away with another perspective on how to deal with various swing problems. Often it may be how to inject humour into the serious aspect of teaching technique, or a completely different approach to curing a common fault.

I am sure that Kitrina's book will benefit everyone – teachers, professionals, high and low handicappers alike – it will certainly be on my bookshelf and I recommend that it is on yours too!

Mickey Walker

Introduction

I have been given a tremendous amount of pleasure from golf as it has given me the opportunity to represent England and Great Britain, which were goals I had from childhood; it has taken me all over the world and given me the opportunity of making friends and meeting terrific characters; it has also been an education and has given me an occupation. I hope this book gives encouragement to those with high handicaps, inspiration to the intermediate golfer and thought for the advanced.

The title of this book, *100 Tips for Lady Golfers*, might promote three questions. Firstly, one hundred, isn't that too many? Far from loving this most noble of games, I have heard some liken it to having a tooth extracted at the dentist's. For something that the majority of golfers do to relax or enjoy as a hobby it seems to me that they are putting themselves through unnecessary torture.

However, advice like 'take a lesson' will probably get the retort 'I only play for fun, I don't want to get serious'. I have never known a country like ours for people boasting that they've 'never had a lesson' – indeed most of them look like it!

The questions I put forward are: Do you enjoy hitting good shots? Do you enjoy sinking long putts? What about making birdies, pars and winning competitions?

If your answer is 'yes' to any of the above then you should realize that to achieve these things you must follow a few basic fundamentals and do a little work. Time spent now will reward you in years to come.

When I started playing golf I knew that there would probably be a difficult and an easy way to learn. I therefore had lessons every week, and in three years my handicap came down from 36 to 14, 14 to 3, 3 to 1. I remember one of the ladies from my club asking me to play a few holes, and when I explained I didn't have time because I was going for a lesson, she exclaimed 'Oh, haven't you learnt yet?'

Well, I am glad to say that I hadn't learnt, and no matter how good I become, I hope I never stop learning. Golf is such a fascinating yet fun game that I am continually learning new shots and gaining a better understanding of the game. Whatever your standard, don't restrict your learning, make the most of it.

One hundred tips isn't a lot, indeed it's the minimum I wanted to start with.

I'm sure I could have written one thousand, and then you might have screamed 'too much!'

The second question from the title is the 'tips'. Is there a difference between a tip and a lesson? I would categorically say, 'Yes there is!'

A tip, as the dictionary explains, is a helpful hint, something that will make a good swing better or channel your thinking; it is not meant to replace your lessons, but to complement them. If you are a beginner, a professional will show you how to grip the club, then maybe how to aim. After you have mastered that you will move on to the stance, then the takeaway and so on. Although you may have been told how to do something, it is not always easy to achieve, and that is where a tip will assist and help you reach your potential.

Throughout this book I hope to give you tips which will sometimes help your swing, at other times your understanding, or give you ways in which to improve the many parts of your golf game.

The world of golf is littered with clichés which for both beginner and layman must be confusing. For example, what is tempo? Is it anything like temper? Is a pivot like a rivet? If you swing in-to-out, will your insides come out? And is your takeaway something you get from the Chinese? Golf is a difficult enough game without having to use the dictionary during your first lesson. Throughout this book I hope to give some explanations. As my subject matter is so vast there are sure to be many things I have missed, so watch out for the thousand tips.

Lastly, as the title indicates, this book is for lady golfers. Many might ask if there is a difference between how ladies and men play golf. Of course there are major differences between the sexes. We have different characteristics, which means generally we ladies will not be as strong as the average male. This fact shouldn't hold any lady back or stop her playing good golf, achieving low scores or having a good swing. However, we all need to acknowledge that there are differences and adapt our game accordingly.

PART ONE

CHAPTER 1

Equipment

 **TIP 1 GETTING STARTED**

With the amount of equipment available for aspiring golfers it is a minefield deciding which makes and models to select. To say that equipment is not important to the beginner is foolhardy; it's like saying that a trainee carpenter can learn with a blunt chisel. The golf club is the golfer's tool and needs to be of good quality.

Over the last few years millions of pounds have been spent in club development which has made it easier to hit the ball. If you have ever seen or tried very old clubs, mashie niblicks, hickory shafts etc., you will know they can be difficult to hit, and I'm glad I don't have to use them now.

Whether it is your first time on the course or you are an experienced professional, the equipment you use is of vital importance. Your age, height, weight, strength and golf ability all have to be taken into consideration.

The flex of the shaft and the club's weight and lie will affect how you swing it. If a club is too upright for you the heel will hit the ground at impact, causing you to hood the face and the ball will go left.

If the club is too flat, the toe will hit the ground at impact, causing the face to open and the ball to go right.

Too heavy a club might cause an overswing and loss of control. If the shaft is too stiff the ball will not fly correctly.

Therefore, unless you know an awful lot about clubs it is better to go to your professional to be 'fitted out'; this might sometimes be more expensive than picking a set at random, but, as with many things, buy in haste, repent at leisure.

It is not necessary for the beginner to have a full set of clubs. The maximum allowed under The R & A Rules is 14 in competition. However, I would advise the beginner to use a 3, 4 or 5 wood and either the

Fig. 1

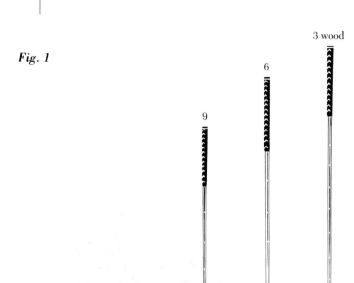

3 wood

6

9

odd or even irons, i.e. 4, 6, 8, or 5, 7, 9. Then include a pitching wedge, sand wedge and putter. Contrary to what many beginners think is logical, the higher the number the shorter the distance the ball will travel.

Each club is a different length; the longer the club, the longer the arc the club makes when you swing, and the faster the clubhead will travel. The more loft on the club face, the higher the ball will go and the quicker it will stop when it lands on the green (see fig. 2). The higher the club's number, the shorter it is (see fig. 1).

Fig. 2

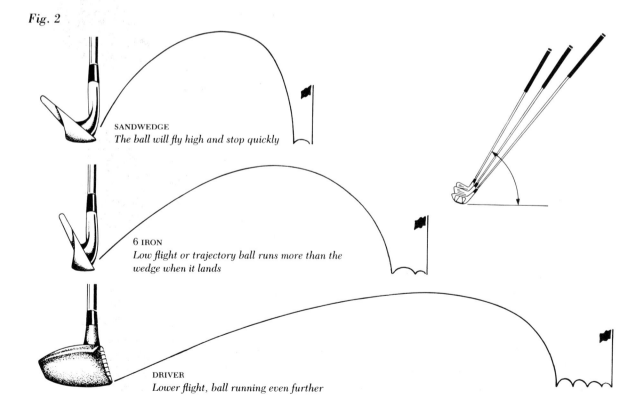

SANDWEDGE
The ball will fly high and stop quickly

6 IRON
Low flight or trajectory ball runs more than the wedge when it lands

DRIVER
Lower flight, ball running even further

TIP 2 · THE BALL

Although many golfers comment on the various advantages one make and construction of ball will have over another, most don't really understand the basic fundamentals of golf ball design and construction. I have heard more misinformation given on balls than on almost any other subject in golf. I wouldn't say that unless you understand golf ball dynamics you shouldn't use a ball (that would be like saying if you don't know the mechanics of a car engine you shouldn't drive a car); however, most of us have a preference for which model we drive based on performance, style, etc., and although not quite as involved, the same can be said of the golf ball. The decision to play a particular ball should not be based on what other people say but rather on what you have found better suited to your game.

I played for a number of years with a ball which had a solid construction and a surlyn cover, and was constantly told by other people that they were not good for chipping or putting. However, I had no problems around the green when using them, and in fact found them more consistent than any other ball.

Over the years since golf was first played, the golf ball has changed dramatically, in size, composition, flight and trajectory.

The history of the golf ball

The earliest balls made were called 'Featheries', so called because they were full of feathers. The outside was made of untanned bull's hide sewn together to make a ball, with a small opening where a top-hatful of feathers was stuffed inside. When dry these balls would go about 180 yards, when wet they would only go 150 yards.

The next development of the golf ball came in the nineteenth century, with the gutta-percha, a ball made from the sap of the gutta-percha tree, which could be softened when heated for moulding and set rock hard when cooled. The advantage with these balls was firstly in cost and secondly in performance. They were not susceptible, as was the feathery, to bursting open when hit.

In the 1890s Dr Coburn Haskell, a dentist from Cleveland, Ohio, experimented with a ball made up of a liquid-filled rubber centre, wound tightly with strips of elastic and covered with gutta-percha.

Today golf is played with a ball very similar to the Haskell ball, although obviously over the years it has been improved and modified.

Most professionals prefer a wound ball with a balata cover, as these have the greatest feel. For the average golfer, balata has been replaced by surlyn, a man-made substance, more durable than the natural rubber, and many amateurs prefer a solid ball as opposed to a wound ball because they go slightly further and last longer.

Which ball you decide to use will depend on your handicap, finances and preference. If you have a high handicap it will only make a slight difference which ball you use. Any golfer who uses a balata cover should be prepared to buy a new ball each time it goes into a bunker or she hits a thinned shot. Lower handicap players should decide how much feel they require versus durability. There are so many differences when deciding which ball to use that I would suggest better players experiment with different balls in contrasting conditions before any final choice is made.

The only suggestion I would make is that a new ball will obviously perform better than any old ball, so use as new a ball as possible when you play, and don't be seduced by the price of an old ball into playing with something that looks as though it came out of the ark.

TIP 3   WEDGES

'Kitrina, why do you carry three wedges in your bag?' is a question I am often asked by golfers peering into my bag. Another look will tell them that I often only carry two woods. However, if you were to take a look into my bag during a practice round, you might think I was a club salesman out on a call. During practice rounds it isn't unusual for me to carry about five wedges, four woods and my normal 2 to 9 irons, plus my putter. So why the additional weapons during practice? Let me explain.

The game of golf is a delicate balance of feel, power, muscle memory and tempo. The closer you get to the green and to the hole, the more accurate you have to be, so the more important it is to make the right decision.

Take for instance the average drive. The fairway you have to aim at is approximately 40 yards wide. When you reach your ball on the fairway, you will be faced with a shot to a green that is 20 yards wide. By the time you reach the green area you are aiming at a hole 4¼ inches wide, therefore the margin for error is much less and so you have to adjust your game to make the most of the shorter shots, i.e. chipping, bunker shots and putting. The old

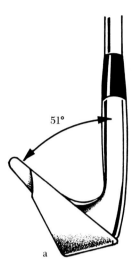

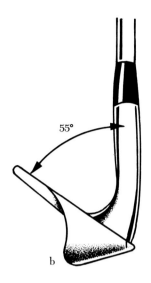

a. Putting wedge

b. Sand wedge. The flange is the large protrusion on the base of the sand wedge, useful for getting the ball out of sand

adage 'Drive for show, putt for dough' is so true.

In my thinking, if I hit a bad drive, I can make up with the next; if I miss a green I can chip close; but if I miss a short putt or fluff a chip I run out of chances. I like to leave my options open, and have the choice of what sort of shot would best suit the circumstances, hence the reason for so many wedges.

The first of my wedges is an old faithful sand wedge, used for chipping from bare lies or for shots that need to be hit very high. The second is the sand wedge which has a large flange and is very good out of most bunkers and for 70-yard shots, but not too good out of very bare lies. Lastly there is my pitching wedge, which I would use to hit chip and run shots around the green and for 70–100 yard shots.

During practice rounds I carry a few trial clubs to see whether they perform better in the prevailing conditions than my regular clubs. Poor caddy, I hear you say. However, it is important to remember that some courses we play have very lush grass, some courses have very tight lies. At some courses the bunkers are filled with powdery sand and at other courses the sand resembles dried mud. If you don't have the club for the job you can't play the shot.

I remember one lady asking me how to play a shot from a very tight lie at the side of a green where her ball usually finished. After showing her how to play the shot, I had a look at the club she'd been trying to use. It was a very heavy sand wedge with the most enormous flange. I explained that the thinned shot she'd been hitting was not entirely her fault – as part of the cause was her equipment. When I let her try my club, there was an immediate improvement in her shots.

If you are not hitting your bunker shots well, or you can't quite master a chip shot, maybe you don't have the right equipment for the job.

Take a look at your clubs and then compare them with other golfers'. Look at what Pros are playing with, and if you can get your hands on their wedge have a look at how it lies on the ground when you address the ball. If you can't keep several clubs for different conditions get one that is fairly good in all conditions. Don't be frightened to wander into the pro shop and have a waggle of the wedges.

THE DRIVER

There are three areas of the game that most professionals look at very closely. They are: putting, shots from around the green and driving.

The tee shot sets up how you play the hole. It is of little use being a great iron player if your drives are invariably in the trees.

The driver is probably the first club you reach for on most holes, and it therefore has to be a friend. If

you are not happy with your driver you are not likely to hit it confidently.

I have several drivers I take away with me, and I'm always on the lookout to see what is new on the market. It might not be that I want to change; however, club development is improving so rapidly, that it would be foolish of me not to try everything, compare it with what I have and then make a decision based on the result.

I feel I need a few drivers with me each week because the courses and the conditions vary so much. On some courses I need carry off the tee, on other courses I want the ball to run and so a low trajectory is required.

It is unrealistic for the average amateur to have several drivers and so it is more important to have a club suited not only to your swing but also to the course on which you play most often.

When considering buying a driver you need to look at both the head and the shaft. The head of the club should not only be pleasing to the eye, but lofted and weighted to suit your standard and strength. I prefer small-headed clubs, but that is simply a preference and it wouldn't stop me using a club with a large head if it hit it better than my own.

The shaft is often overlooked when ladies are considering buying clubs. There are many different types of shaft, steel, graphite, boron, titanium, etc. There are the low and high torques and a vast choice of swing flex. This might sound complicated, but all this information and technology is so that we hit the ball with the club that suits our characteristics. Since we are all different shapes, sizes and strengths it is logical that the shafts we use are slightly different.

The choice of makes and models is almost innumerable. What is important is getting it right for your game and the course you are to play. Experimenting with new clubs shouldn't be something to be feared or dreaded, it should be fun, even if it's only to confirm that the clubs you are using are superior!

TIP 5 — ADJUST YOUR PUTTER TO SUIT YOUR SET UP

The putter is without doubt the most used piece of equipment in your golf bag, and I would say that the putter is the most important club in the bag.

All cars are built to standard specifications. When the driver gets into a car the seat is adjusted to the required leg length, the seat back to the most comfortable position, the mirrors and steering wheel get al-

tered to individual needs. Unfortunately, when you buy a golf club it is not so easy to make adjustments as in the car. However, the same reasoning still applies: we are all different heights, leg and arm lengths, and to get something comfortable, we must alter it slightly.

Modern manufacturing techniques make it prohibitively expensive to offer a wide range of lengths for putters. Some companies offer more choice of length than others, but that is still not enough to fit every golfer's putting stance. Some short people bend over a lot and need a very short putter, others want extra length, and so on.

I have been using the same putter for the last ten years, and one of the first things I did was to cut three inches off the top of the shaft. I am 5ft 9 inches tall, and if I had to shorten my putter, I would think it possible that a great many lady golfers should do the same. If the putter is sticking into your stomach, or catching your sweater as you address the putt then it is certainly too long.

It is important in putting to have as much control as possible, and if your putter is too long you will not be able to stand comfortably to the ball. By reducing the length of your putter you will gain more control and be able to keep a firm stroke whilst putting.

TIP 6 CLUB MAINTENANCE

It never ceases to amaze me the number of golfers who try to play golf with shiny grips and dirty clubfaces. Golf club manufacturers have spent years producing designs which make it easier to get lift and backspin, and clubs are delicately balanced with an exact swing weight. However, all this modern technology is neutralized when the clubface is caked in mud, because the club will not perform as it is supposed to.

It is simply not good enough to drop your clubs in the boot of your car until next week. Woods left in the car when wet, with the clubhead cover on, will quickly deteriorate. Irons with nicks in the faces can begin to corrode, as can the shafts. Golf grips become clogged and very shiny unless frequently cleaned (especially if you use hand cream regularly!)

Perhaps the equipment I should have included here are a towel, scrubbing brush and shoe cleaner.

Cleaning only takes a couple of minutes, and if you get into a routine of cleaning each time you play it will be a lot easier.

Make sure you clean the grooves, scrub the grips and keep your clubs dry when not being used. Once a year it is a good idea to change your grips. If you can't afford a new set of grips, try taking a piece of sandpaper and gently rubbing the grip to bring back the texture. You can't expect to keep a firm hold of the club with shiny grips.

If you have wooden woods, they need to be varnished to protect the wood, and the whipping needs to be tight to prevent cracking around the neck.

If you have graphite shafts, make sure they are protected. Some golf bags have sheep skin around the club dividers, which protects shafts. Woods should have the long head covers which go a good way down the shaft.

If you have spent a lot of time and money getting a good set of clubs together, make the most of them! Club maintenance must become part of your golf routine. Remember the old adage 'If you look after your clubs they will look after you!'

CHAPTER 2

Basics

 **THE GRIP**

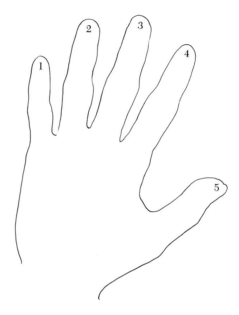

I remember as a child singing at Sunday School how the wise man built his house upon the rock. In the golf swing how you hold the club will either give you the opportunity to improve quickly or can possibly hold you back and cause an array of bad shots.

If you want to build your golf swing on a solid rock you must persevere and grip the club correctly. Beginners often feel that they have extra fingers when trying to grip the club for the first time. More experienced players used to a grip that is strong or weak will often say the correct grip feels too uncomfortable for them to change.

For the swing to work properly the hands must be in a position that will allow a correct wrist cock, and a square hit at the ball with maximum power.

There are five check points in my grip, one for each finger on my right hand, and at the beginning of the year I always go through my check list, to make sure I haven't lapsed into bad habits.

The check points are as follows:

1 The golf club handle should be held diagonally across the left hand as shown overleaf. I can hold the club in only these three fingers if necessary.
2 The fingers should then close around the club.

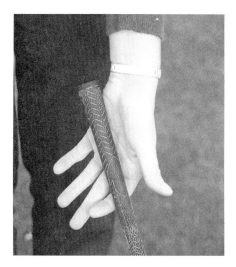

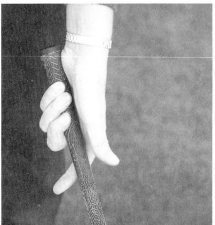

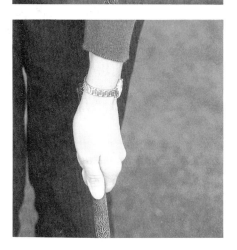

3 The left thumb is then placed on the club.

4 When I place my right hand on the club my main thought is that I want the palm of my right hand to face the target at address and impact. I actually check this all through the season, and when I line up I point my right palm down the fairway in the direction I want the ball to go. My left palm is obviously further up the shaft, but if I were to bring them together they would be palm to palm.

5 I then have the thumb and index finger of my right hand pressed firmly together. I try to think of my hands as one unit, gripping the club with equal pressure. My hands will not be loose

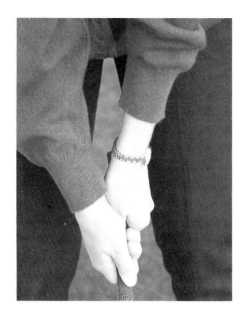

enough for the club to be pulled out, and they will not be holding the club so tightly that my wrists and forearms become rigid.

WHETHER YOU INTERLOCK, OVERLAP OR HAVE A TWO-FISTED GRIP IS A MATTER FOR EACH INDIVIDUAL. THERE IS A MUCH HIGHER PERCENTAGE OF PLAYERS WHO USE THE OVERLAPPING GRIP; HOWEVER, THERE HAVE BEEN TOP PLAYERS WHO HAVE USED EACH METHOD.

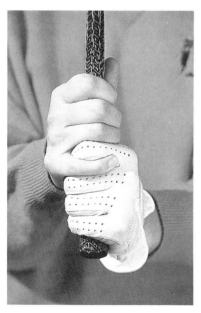

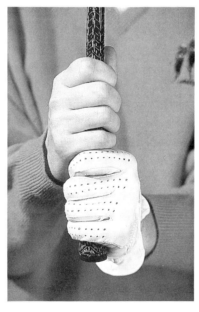

Varden Grip (Little finger on right hand overlaps index finger on left hand)

Two fisted grip (NOT BASEBALL)

Interlocking grip (Little finger on right hand interlocks with index finger on left hand as shown)

POSITIONING THE BALL

POSITIONING THE CLUBHEAD behind the ball accurately and AIMING THE CLUBHEAD at the target, are two things which many beginners overlook, often because they are so preoccupied with hitting the ball or concentrating on trying to swing the club.

If the ball isn't centred in the middle of the clubface it will be difficult to hit the ball out of the middle, and if the clubhead is not facing the target, the ball will not fly towards it.

If you take a look at different clubheads you will notice that the head size will vary between manufacturers, and each clubhead size will vary depending on the loft of the club. Most clubheads are roughly 4 inches by 2 inches and shaped in a way that has been developed to make the ball go up in the air. A correctly hit shot will go further if it is hit out of the middle of the club, than if it is hit out of either the toe or the heel. This middle spot is called the SWEET SPOT. If you miss the middle and hit either side, it will make a different sound – obviously not so sweet!

The beginner should pay attention to making sure the ball is in front of the sweet spot when placing the club behind the ball.

Try hitting a few shots from the toe of the club. Notice any difference in sound and feel? Then hit a few from out of the heel to feel the difference. Finally hit a few shots from the middle of the club and listen for the difference in sound that it makes. If you practise this drill a few times you should be able to tell where the ball hit the clubface by how it felt, and the sound that it made.

THE ACTUAL MIDDLE OF THE CLUBFACE IS MIDWAY BETWEEN THE TOE OF THE CLUB AND THE HOSEL, THIS IS SLIGHTLY TOWARDS THE HEEL OF THE CLUB. IF YOU LOOK AT A GOOD PLAYER'S CLUBS THERE WILL BE WEAR NEARER THE HEEL THAN THE TOE. THE BEGINNER SHOULD TRY TO HIT THE BALL FROM THE MIDDLE OF THE CLUB FACE AND NOT TOO CLOSE TO THE HOSEL AS THERE WILL BE A DANGER OF SHANKING THE BALL.

CLUBHEAD AIM

We have already established the reasons for getting the clubhead directly behind the ball. It is also important to position the clubface so that it is aimed at the target.

The bottom of the clubface is the part that should be lined up with the target. When placing the clubface behind the ball, the bottom of the club should be perpendicular to the ball-to-target line.

Most beginners find it difficult to align the face of the club with something 100 yards away, but you can't expect to hit the ball at the target if the clubface isn't aiming at it. It will certainly get easier with a little practice. If you want to check that the clubface is aiming correctly, take your stance and aim the club at the target. Then get a friend to hold your club still while you stand behind on line with the target, where it is easier to see exactly where the face is aligned.

Another way the beginner might check how the clubface is aiming is to mark a line on the grass aiming at the target, then make sure that the line forms a 90 degree angle with the middle leading edge of the club.

In the same way that you learnt to differentiate between the middle and sides of the clubhead, you can learn to tell which way the clubface is aiming. First open the clubface to the right, see what effect it has when you hit the ball with the face in that direction, then hood or close the face so that it is aiming left. Hit some shots and see the effect it has on the ball. Finally put the clubface squarely behind the ball aiming at the target and hit a few shots.

Paying attention to detail might seem tedious, but if you get into good habits to begin with it will save you hitting a lot of wild shots.

> THE BALL-TO-TARGET LINE IS AN IMAGINARY LINE GOING FROM THE BALL TO THE TARGET. SEE TIP 12.

LINING UP

It is often said by many teaching professionals that over 70 per cent of faults occur before the club has even been taken back from the ball. Faults in aim, grip and ball position are just as damaging as not keeping your head still or bending your left arm too much during your backswing.

Many golfers I watch are so eager to get on and hit the ball that the correct aim is forgotten, resulting in swing faults.

If you are not aiming at the target, your mind will send a signal telling your body, for example, that it's aiming thirty yards off line; your body will then try to get the ball to go to the target, which normally results in the most peculiar movements whilst you wrestle with your swing trying to get the ball on line.

Surely it's much easier to spend a fraction more time to start with, making sure your body is lined up, and save yourself these headaches.

If you have the opportunity to watch professionals lining up before hitting a shot, one of the things you will notice is how they take time to make sure everything is correct before starting to swing.

You will very rarely see a professional just rush up, grab a club, look at the target and hit. No, we discipline ourselves to go through the line-up procedure even when we are really confident that we could aim without doing so.

Unfortunately golf is a game where, to get the best results, you must be disciplined. If you prefer to hit greens more often then, as I explained earlier, pay attention to this detail and you will enjoy your golf more as a result.

Here is a tip to check your aim:

On the practice ground or even on the golf course, if you are not playing in a competition, you will find it helpful to place two clubs on the ground.

The first club should be aimed directly at the target. Put it on the far side of the ball where it will help you to visualize the direction that the ball and clubhead will travel. The second club is placed parallel to the first to align your feet, shoulders and hips.

If you are playing in a competition, you can use a club on the course for lining up. However, you must, according to rule 8-2, lift any

> OFTEN GOLFERS TRY TO AIM THEIR SHOULDERS, HIPS AND FEET STRAIGHT AT THE TARGET, WHEN IN FACT THEY SHOULD BE AIMING PARALLEL TO THE BALL-TO-TARGET LINE. IF YOU LINE YOUR BODY UP WITH THE TARGET YOU WILL ACTUALLY BE AIMING TO THE RIGHT.

artificial aid before making your shot, or in stroke play you will incur a 2-stroke penalty, and in match play loss of hole. It is, therefore, usually too much hassle for a player to put a club down during competitions, as by the time the club has been picked up, the correct line up will have changed.

There are, however, ways to check on your alignment and not break the rules.

The way I line up is probably the most common method, and one I would advise every golfer to try: –

Stand behind your ball, so that the ball is directly between you and the target. Imagine an invisible line going straight from your ball to the target. Now pick out something on that line, a few inches in front of the ball. Make sure that you are able to see that spot clearly when you move round to take up your stance. Keeping your eyes on that spot, firstly align your clubhead with it, secondly take your grip, then line up your feet and shoulders.

TIP 11 · STANCE

The posture and stance you adopt in your set-up will affect the way you swing the club, and it is therefore very important that you get this right. There are three things that need attention: your head position, your shoulders and the lower part of your body.

Head up

Have you ever been told to 'Keep your head down'? I am amazed at the number of lady golfers who have been told to keep their heads down, often by well-meaning husbands. However, it is probably the worst piece of golf advice you will have ever been given, and unfortunately it's probably the most frequently used.

It is impossible to turn your shoulders whilst at the same time burying your head in your chest. In fact what normally happens when told to keep your head down is that the whole of your body lifts up because it's trying to turn and can't. The more you try to keep your head down, the more likely you are to lift your head and the rest of your body with it!

What you want to think is – **head up, head still**. Your head, and in particular your chin, has to be up

away from your chest or you will not be able to turn your shoulders correctly. Your head has to be still so that you can turn your body around it. If you move your head to the right as you swing back, it's not likely that it will move on its own – your shoulders will probably move back as well. If they move back from the ball and stay back you will hit the ground behind the ball.

TIP 12 · WHERE DO ALL THE SHOTS COME FROM?

Bad shots – what makes them happen? Where do they come from? Are they really your fault? Many golfers don't believe that they are their fault, thinking them to be a little like the weather; they just come out of the blue!

Every time you hit a ball, the way it flies and the direction it goes will tell you much about the way it has been hit. Learning to understand this will really help your understanding of the swing.

There are two factors which affect the direction of the ball:

1 The direction your swing is going.
2 The direction the clubhead is aiming when you hit the ball.

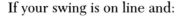

If your swing is on line and:

A: the club aims to the left, the shot will go left.
B: the club aims to the target, the ball will go to the target.
C: the club aims to the right, the shot will go to the right.

If you take the club inside the ball-to-target line in the backswing, thus having an in-to-out swing, and:

A: the club aims to the left, you will hook the ball.
B: the club aims at the target, you will draw the ball.
C: the club aims to the right, you will hit the ball straight right.

If you take the club back outside the ball-to-target line in the backswing, thus swinging out-to-in, and:

A: the club aims to the left, you will hit the ball left.
B: the club aims to the target, you will hit a fade.
C: the club aims to the right, you will hit a slice.

THE BALL-TO-TARGET LINE IS AN IMAGINARY LINE EXTENDING FROM THE BALL TO THE TARGET.

2. *Stand with arms straight out, butt end of club aimed at navel, then bend from hips*

4. *Bend from waist incorrect*

5. *Bend from hips correct*

TIP 13 Bend from the hips

When you move the top part of your body forward to address the ball, it must be a bend from the hips, and not from the waist. One sure way of getting a bad back is to bend from the waist, which puts tremendous pressure on your back during your swing. Ideally, you should keep your back as straight as possible. If you can visualize your spine running down your back when you swing it should be like a pole, with your shoulders rotating around it.

If your arms are too close to your body you will not be able to turn properly, and if they are too far away you will fall forward.

Take hold of a club, stand up straight with your arms straight out in front of you at shoulder height, shoulders back, and back straight. Lower your arms so that the butt end of the club is pointing at your navel, then bend forward from your hips until the club touches the ground.

From this position you can turn your hips and shoulders easily, your arms are a comfortable distance from your body and your head can stay still.

Flex your knees

Over the years there have been many opposing views on how your knees should work. Some say keep them straight, others say sit on a bar stool. However, I can't see either of these being correct. I don't play golf sitting down; if you were to sit down whilst trying to play golf, you would not allow your hips to turn, which would restrict your shoulder turn.

What I think we are looking for is a slight bend forward of the knees so that your hips can turn. Imagine that your knees are going to point at your toes.

The correct distance that your feet are apart will vary from golfer to golfer. Basically if they are too wide, you will not be able to turn your hips in the backswing, and if they are too close to each other, you will fall over when you swing.

TIP 14 BASICS FOR JUNIORS

Kids make the best natural golfers. I love watching the wee girls who turn up to the Gloucestershire County encouragement days. Seeing the eleven-year-olds swat the ball is great.

We are fortunate that the game of golf spans the generations. It must be very rewarding for a granny to introduce her granddaughter to a game that is played all around the world, by all ages and social positions.

However, there are pitfalls when bringing children into this game, with its antiquated traditions, the etiquette rules and the 'do's' and 'don'ts' that every golf club has.

The two most important things for junior golfers are to get the clubs

Three young golfers at an encouragement day

they use cut down to their own size, and to take them to a professional for lessons. If you have had a swing fault all your life for goodness' sake don't pass it on to them!

The grip, stance, posture and set-up are important whatever your age. However, most youngsters have a short concentration span, and too much 'coaching' will either confuse them or go in one ear and out the other. The best way to teach kids is to let them watch the pros either live at a tournament or on television. Let them become enthused by watching the greats and learn from the best how to swing.

The hardest thing for adults to do is keep their mouths buttoned up!

When I started playing golf countless well-meaning people kept telling me what was wrong with my swing. The only effect they had was to undermine my confidence and make me concentrate on the negative parts of my game. If someone is having lessons, let the teacher tell them what is wrong with their swing, and if they are not having lessons then give them some really worthwhile advice: tell them to

start! Perhaps if you really want to help then you could pay for their coaching.

One of the best pieces of advice my father ever gave me was: be polite and then forget everything anyone but your coach says. I still find that advice helpful today!

Lastly, it's no good forcing kids to do something they don't want to, they will only hate golf if you push them too much. It is a wise parent who lets a child develop at her own speed, and if the inclination and desire to be a good player is there, she will put the hours in.

TIP 15 — WHAT TO DO WITH YOUR CHEST

If you are not well endowed you probably have no understanding of the problems many women face when they set up to the golf ball.

Do I swing "under" or "over" is a question I am often asked. I have to answer, neither really.

If you set up with your arms above your chest, it will mean you are firstly standing too far away from the ball and secondly that you will swing too upright.

If you set up under your chest, you will not stand to the ball correctly and are likely to swing too flat.

You need to set up to the ball so that your left arm dissects your left breast, running diagonally across it.

If you are able to stand up straight and hold the club at arm's length then you should be able to do the same at the ball. The reason women with larger chests have a problem is that they don't turn their shoulders, but allow their arms to move across their chests, which is where, if you have a large bosom, you get stuck.

The second problem larger women face is their balance. If they bend too far forward to make room, they will fall forward. The set-up position is therefore much more important to these women. You will find it helpful to stick your bottom out so that you don't fall forward, and really concentrate on turning your shoulders and cocking your wrists, not staying still and moving your arms.

CHAPTER 3

The Swing

 **THE TURN**

It has been my experience that although the turn away from the ball and through to the target might seem easy, golfers get very confused, and in particular women confuse a turn and a tilt.

I have said that the whole point of the swing is to get the ball from where it is to where you want it to be, and this is achieved by backward and forward movements in the swing, part of which is your turn.

In the backswing your hips and shoulders turn away from the ball and the weight moves on to your right side. In the down and through swing they almost repeat the movement facing the other side, your hips and shoulders turn through to the target and your weight moves on to your left side. However, knowing what happens often makes beginners more confused. When you learn to walk no one describes what each muscle and ligament does in order for you to put one foot in front of the other, neither do you dwell on wrist rotation when you learn to skip. Unfortunately, as we get older we become fixated by HOW we do things. In order to get a more relaxed and natural turn, try this movement without using a club.

Stand with your feet about eighteen inches apart and imagine someone has called to you from behind. How would you turn? You would look over your right shoulder, rotating hips, shoulders and head to the right, your weight would naturally transfer from the centre to the right, and your left heel might be pulled off the ground slightly by the rotation of your hips. Now suppose someone then called to you from the other side, you would turn round and face the other direction, looking over the left side, your weight distribution would move from being mostly on the right side to mostly on the left, and you would finish with hips, shoulders and head in the other direction.

Look over your right shoulder then the left. Now try making the same movement but with a still head.

This is how your body should work in the golf swing. It's not a manufactured movement but a very simple turn. Now try the same exercise, keeping your head facing forward as you would in the golf swing and try focusing your eyes on an imaginary ball on the ground. Keep your head still and make the same turn with your hips and shoulders and weight, first to the right as you would in your backswing and then through to the other side as you would in your follow through. Learning the proper body movement need not be difficult, and if you try this a few times around the house you will find the turn easier to reproduce during play.

TIP 17 — SHORTEN YOUR SWING

Golfers often get confused as to what is an overswing and what is a long swing.

The first sign of what might be an **overswing** is when the club drops below horizontal at the top of the backswing as in illustration b. Some golfers can even see the clubhead out of the corner of their left eye.

There are several reasons for overswinging and the most common is a loose grip which allows the club to drop down at the top of the swing.

Other causes include rolling the clubface open in the backswing, bending your left arm severely, and tilting instead of turning your body.

A long swing differs from an overswing in that it is not necessarily an incorrect swing, and although the left arm is straight and the grip is firm, the golfer is supple enough to swing beyond what is normally acceptable at the top, or finish, of the back swing. One reason for ladies overswinging is a lack of strength – most women can't hold their left arm and club in place, and instead of them swinging the club, the club swings them! If the club is too heavy it will just go where it wants.

Women are much more supple than men and generally not muscle-bound so there are a larger number of women who have long swings compared to men. Junior golfers often, because they have young bones and very supple bodies, swing very full and long, but as they get older and stronger their swings shorten naturally.

Whilst having a long swing is not necessarily an obvious problem, it does make it difficult to hit the ball hard whilst keeping your rhythm, and if you play in the wind with a long swing it will be affected more than a shorter firm swing. If you can keep your swing just below horizontal at the top it will give you more

a

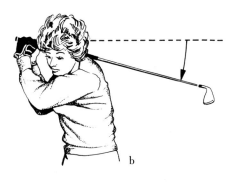

b

try this they think they are stopping at the top, when in fact they are just continuing straight down. To make sure you stop, try counting 1, 2, 3 before you allow your self to swing back down. If you totally mis-hit the ball don't worry, your co-ordination will get better the more you practise, and at the end of the day it is only a practice, you don't have to swing like this whilst playing. Practising doing this will not only encourage you to swing shorter but will also build strength and help your co-ordination.

a. Correct

b. Incorrect

control and help you to hit your shots crisply, as shown in illustration a.

If you want to shorten your swing slightly, any small change that you make will feel enormous, so to begin with, try swinging back three-quarters of your back swing and stop completely. Hold it there for a couple of seconds before swinging down. When I ask some golfers to

 ## TIP 18 GETTING YOUR SHOULDERS TO TURN

No one part of the swing is more important than any other, and no one part of the swing will make you hit the ball further. It is a joint effort in which every part of the swing goes towards helping you to hit the ball, right from your head, which centres your body, to your feet, which keep you balanced and allow a turn. If you try to make one part of your body move faster, i.e. your legs, it will become unbalanced.

Women have a lazy habit of not turning their shoulders in the back-swing because it is easier just to pick the club up. Nevertheless, for building a good backswing it is vital that the shoulders turn fully. If they do not turn then other parts of the body compensate for the lack of turn, i.e. your arms will become over-active and swing back too far.

What some golfers think is turning the shoulders can be a tilt.

To help develop a good shoulder turn, first hold a club straight out in

front of you at about waist height, using your shoulders to promote the turn. Draw an imaginary line around your body with the clubhead whilst turning to the right. Once you have reached 90 degrees, stop and go back the other way through 180 degrees. You can turn your hips a little to enable your shoulders to turn. Try this for a few swings very slowly, stopping either side. Then try it a little faster, building up to the tempo at which you would normally swing the club.

Next try the same thing but add a wrist cock to the movement. Once again, start slowly and build up to the tempo of your swing.

I swing like this for a few minutes

before nearly every practice session and especially if I'm not playing regularly or my muscles feel a little tight. It helps make sure that my shoulders are turning, as when I am standing straight up it is very easy to make a big turn.

Hold club upside down

TIP 19

LEARN TO RELAX

A golfer's swing can range from the most beautiful fluid movement to an awkward rigid jerk. There are so many moving parts in the swing that you cannot afford to be tense or rigid and expect to swing properly.

It is surprising the number of people I play with who, in a matter of seconds, go from being quite re-laxed in their muscles to being com-pletely rigid. Instead of holding their arms out in a relaxed but firm position, they stretch their arms taut and lock the elbows. Their forearms become stiff and their shoulders hunch up, but this is not the way to attempt to hit the golf ball. In fact, if you lock your elbows you'll probably get tennis elbow.

We all get nervous and tense at times, but this is something we must learn to cope with. The first thing that normally happens when we are tense is that our shoulders move up and closer together. Therefore, if

Swish it back and through

you are nervous or feel tense, make a conscious effort to push your shoulders down and back.

Most people rush things when they are nervous, they talk more quickly; nervous golfers swing the club more quickly and take less time lining up before they hit. If you are in a tense situation, make sure you slow everything down. Think things through clearly. More silly mistakes are made when golfers are in trouble than at any other time. Why? Because they don't think clearly and take their time, because they are nervous.

You might find it useful to swing a club holding it upside down, below the head instead of the grip, and swish it back and through with a half swing as quickly as you can. Joanne Carner, one of the most successful players of the American Ladies Tour, used to do this when she felt she was tense.

Lastly, when you get over the ball think, relax, take a look at your arms and hands. If your hands have turned white and your forearms are rigid, you are too tense! If this is the case, step back from the ball, give your arms a shake and relax before stepping back to hit your shot.

TIP 20
USE THE WALL

Using a wall as a practice aid has two benefits. Firstly, it is a great way to understand how your body works through the ball and a check that it is performing correctly.

At address, your hands, arms, shoulders, hips and legs are all together, but as you start to swing back it is very easy for one part of your body to move more quickly or slowly than it should. If your shoulders move back before the rest of your body they will probably come back into the ball before the rest, and at impact your hands will be so far behind that it will be impossible to hit the ball properly. At impact it is important to get a square hit, with each part of your body working at the right speed in relation to the rest. It is important to realize that there is very little difference between your address position and your impact position. The only difference is that at impact your shoulders, hips and hands are a fraction in front of their address position.

To get the feeling of the square impact position, stand with the bottom of your club shaft against a wall. If you have enough room, go to the top of your swing and come down slowly to the impact position. Press your hands, arms and body forward in the direction that they would normally go to the target; however, do not let them go past the wall.

When you come back to the impact position, if the body is in a very different place to your set-up position it will mean that your body timing is not good. Continue to practise until you return to the correct position.

Secondly, a wall can strengthen your hands and arms in the hitting area. Simply take your stance and hold the clubhead so that it is against the wall. Gently try to turn your body forward as if you were going to follow through but can't, because the wall is there. Hold this taut position against the wall for a couple of minutes. The muscles you are using here are those which are used in hitting the ball, and by trying this every now and then they will be strengthened.

FOLLOW THROUGH

Most of our thoughts are concentrated on set up and backswing and the many movements involved in these parts of the swing, and it becomes easy to forget the follow through once the ball has been hit. Although it might seem that the follow through is an unnecessary appendage tagged on to the important parts of the swing, the follow through is important.

Unless you continue moving your body out of the way as you move through the ball, it will prohibit the smooth acceleration necessary in a good golf swing.

You can learn a lot about your swing by the way you follow through. For instance, if you fall over after you have hit the ball, it indicates that you are unbalanced; if you fall back on your right leg, the cause is probably a reversed pivot.

Practising your follow through is nearly as important as practising your backswing because it's all part of THE SWING, which starts as soon as you take the club back and finishes at the completion of your follow through. It does not stop at the ball, for it did the ball wouldn't go very far.

Simply going to the top of your follow through is useful, don't even take a back swing. Address the ball then slowly turn through to an imaginary target and hold the finish of your follow through.

If you just follow through it is easier to isolate what is making the turn through the ball and what muscles are used in that part of the swing.

Whilst holding the follow through position for a minute, check where your hips have finished. They should be facing the target. Check where your hands and arms have stopped, and where your weight is. Is it on your left or right leg, or both legs? Has your right foot come off the ground? And where is your head facing? Where are your shoulders pointing, and are your knees still flexed? I wonder if you could stand like that for a long time or would you fall over?

After you have practised the follow through without the backswing and know where your hips, shoulders, arms and hands should be, have a few full swings and notice whether you actually do finish in the position that you want.

Maybe you have never thought about your follow through, it just happens. I would agree that a good follow through originates from a good backswing, and that to a certain extent it is a mirror of the backswing. However, it must still be learnt and practised.

There is a time to focus on your backswing and a time to focus on the through swing.

TIP 22   LEFT ARM

The importance of keeping a straight left arm is stressed by teachers and instruction books almost to the point that many golfers think it is a rigid left arm that is being taught. Keeping a rigid left arm will only do one thing – give you a pain in the elbow.

If you solely focus on a straight left arm you are missing the point.

The reason for setting up with your arm straight is to obtain width. When you set up to the ball your hands are an arm's length from your shoulders, and if a line were drawn down through your body it would show that your hands are roughly in line with the middle of your shoulders. During your swing, if you are to maintain the width your hands and arms should stay the same distance from your shoulders as when they started. You can't gain width in your backswing, the only width you have is the distance from your shoulders to your hands. If you try and gain width in your backswing, you will probably only be swaying or moving off the ball. You can lose width, however, if your left arm bends a lot or if your arms swing independently to your shoulders.

If your shoulders don't turn correctly in your backswing then your arms are likely to try and make up for the lack of turn by moving back and across your chest; your left arm will bend and you will have lost width. However, simply concentrating on keeping that left arm straight will not solve the problem.

Try concentrating on keeping your hands the same distance away from your shoulders as when they started, and start your backswing with your shoulders and arms. At the top of your backswing, don't allow your arms to keep going back as far as they can, try to hold them so that they stay in the middle of your shoulders.

Closed

Open

Correct

LEARN THE CORRECT WRIST COCK

TIP 23

At the many ladies' clinics I give throughout the country there is one thing that more people get wrong and do not understand than any

other, and that is a correct wrist cock. At least half the ladies roll their wrists, opening or closing the clubface when they take the club back. If you do this you have not cocked the wrists at all. Other ladies hinge or cup their left wrists, which can lead to injuries.

If you don't cock your wrists in your backswing you will lose power and distance.

Many women have very long swings. WHen combined with a hinged wrist it is almost impossible to accelerate into the ball. This results in a decelerated downswing and a flick at the ball. In this flicking the right hand overtakes the left producing a thinned shot.

To get the feeling of a wrist cock, simply hold a club at arm's length, with the club pointing straight out away from your body and with the butt end pointing at your stomach. Moving only your wrists, bring the clubhead up towards your head as far as your wrists will comfortably allow. The club has probably gone through 90 degrees, and your wrists have cocked to allow this to happen. This movement is all that happens in your swing. What makes the wrist cock difficult to perform is the fact that you are breaking or cocking your wrists whilst turning your shoulders and body.

To get that action right during your swing try the wristwatch drill.

 ## WATCH YOUR WATCH

It is not only cupping or hingeing your wrists that prevents your arms and wrists making the correct movements in your backswing, rolling your wrists will also have a detrimental effect.

If you roll the clubface open or closed during your backswing, it will be difficult to produce a consistent firm square hit to the back of the ball when you return to the impact position. In order to keep your wrists moving back correctly try watching your watch.

The angle between the back of your left hand and wrist should stay almost the same during the swing. Halfway through your backswing, at around hip height, the watch on your left wrist should be facing at 90 degrees to the fairway. If your watch is pointing towards the sky, it will mean you have opened the clubface. If your watch is facing the ground you will have closed the club face.

Take a few half swings and try to feel where your watch is pointing during your backswing. Concentrate on this whilst practise swinging and then try it whilst hitting balls.

A good shoulder turn and correct

wrist cock are essential if you are going to hit the ball with the accelerated swing needed to hit the ball a long way. Once you understand how your arms and hands work during the swing it is easier to put it into action.

CHAPTER 4

The Warm Up

 **TIP 25** **WARM UP EXERCISES**

One of the most common causes of bad backs and injured muscles among golfers is that they do not 'WARM UP'. Many attempt to rush from work, dash to the first tee and try to hit a long drive.

If you compare golf with other sports, this lack of warm up is very noticeable. How often do you see a runner put on track shoes and start sprinting immediately? If you play tennis or squash, would you walk straight on to the court and start the first set without first having a few warm-up rallies? No, you spend a few minutes warming up, going through your strokes, stretching your muscles and preparing to play.

Why is it we golfers don't see the need to warm up?

Why do I see at least half the players in the Saturday medals tee off without more than a practice putt?

The reason many golfers don't think they need to warm up is that GOLF is not perceived to be an ATHLETIC sport. Most people think of it as a slow sport, a game you take up when you get old.

The common thought is that sprinters move quickly and need to warm up, so do tennis and squash players. This reasoning is not totally correct.

Of course we don't run around, but neither does a discus thrower, yet think of the explosion of power when the discus is launched through the air. It is similar when you wind up in the backswing and then hit down and through the ball.

Think about the golf clubhead. It is moving at anything from fifty to a hundred miles an hour. That's pretty quick, certainly quicker than the tennis racket! The clubhead is being propelled by your hands and body using a variety of muscles, sinews and tendons. A tremendous strain is put on your body when you hit a ball, and if you don't prepare your body correctly, an injury is a possibility.

For most golfers, the time spent at the club is for relaxing. Many golfers simply don't have the time to hit balls as I would do before a tournament round, or they just don't want to.

I understand these problems. However, it's 'no good shutting the stable door after the horse has bolted'. By this I mean, it's too late once you have hurt your back, or injured yourself. Are there any options? Yes. There are several things you can do to warm your muscles up, some of which are described in the next few pages. Deciding which one is best for your lifestyle is up to you. The important thing here, though, is that you do SOMETHING to warm up.

STRETCHING
TIP 26

Gently stretching and loosening your muscles before play is the best way to start your warm up. These stretches need not necessarily be done at the golf club. There are several players I know on the women's tour who do stretching exercises in their hotel rooms before they got to the golf course. I often see girls in the locker room limbering up before they go out to practise prior to play,

and then there are those who do a few stretches before they start hitting practice shots on the practice ground.

The exercises used to stretch vary slightly from player to player. The rule is gently to stretch and warm the muscles you are about to use in the golf swing. But note, there are not a lot of muscles that you don't use.

If you feel embarrassed about warming up at the golf club I suggest you start your warm up at home.

Start by sitting on the floor, legs straight out in front of you. Put your left hand on your right knee, and your right hand about a foot behind your back. Gently turn the top half of your body to the right and hold this position for a few seconds. Then do the same the opposite way round.

I like to start with a few side bends. This obviously involves the muscles in your side and lower back. With your hands either on your hips or by your sides, keep your hips still and bend to the side from your waist, stretch first to the right, keeping your back and shoulders straight, and then to the left; repeat this a few times.

Next, the turn. Place each hand on the opposite shoulder. Keeping your head looking straight forward and your hips facing forwards, turn your shoulders slowly to the right and hold for a couple of seconds, then turn to the left. Do this four or five times.

Put a club behind your shoulders and take a regular golf stance with the rest of your body, then turn your shoulders slowly as you would in your golf swing, first to the right and then to the left as you would when swinging a golf club.

Keeping the club behind your back, and your legs and back straight, bend forward from your hips, hold for a couple of seconds and release.

SWING SLOWLY TO GET READY

The next part of the warm-up routine is swinging the club slowly without hitting any balls, which is the technique that most golfers are likely to have tried at some time or another.

There are very few golfers who wouldn't have a practice swing on the first tee, and with a little thought, and another few minutes of your time, you can really loosen your muscles.

Swing a club, but at about one-tenth of your normal speed, gently stretching your muscles for a few swings.

Then with the same club, swing to the top of your backswing and stop. Hold this position for about ten seconds. You should feel the muscles in your shoulders, arms, back and legs. Try this two or three times.

Swinging two clubs is another good way of warming up. Take two clubs, put the heads together on the ground and grip both grips with your hands. If you have small hands you will not be able to have a proper grip whilst holding two clubs, but as near a normal grip as possible will suffice. Swing normally with the two clubs. They will probably feel quite heavy. Try this for a dozen or so swings.

The most important things to remember with all these warm-up drills is that they should be done very gently and slowly. If you swing too quickly you might pull or tear your muscles. Avoid jerky, unrhythmical movements. When stretching don't wait for it to hurt before you stop. Go as far back in your swing as you can easily, maybe turning your shoulders a little bit further with each successive swing. It is important that you don't overdo the warm up, especially if it is new for you.

TIP 28 · ON THE PRACTICE GROUND

Although many golfers say that when they hit balls on the practice ground they would call it 'PRACTISING' there is definitely a difference between the balls you hit prior to play, and those you hit after play.

Before a round of golf you want to keep your mind clear from thoughts about technique or swing problems. You should be as positive as possible. Therefore the balls you hit before play are for warm up only, not to work on your swing or correct faults, etc. . . .

After you have finished playing is the time you should think about what went wrong on the course, and about your technique. It is also the time for a lesson or to work on your feel.

Probably the only thing to work on before play is your TEMPO. You might find it helpful to have what the professionals call a 'SWING THOUGHT'.* But too many thoughts will only confuse, and stop you focusing on the important aspects of the game.

When you are warming up on the practice ground the best club to start with is the one you find easiest to hit. Don't, as I see so many people do, go

*See glossary

straight for the driver. I start by hitting a few wedges. The reason I choose a wedge is that it's an easy club to hit, and I can start by hitting half swings and shorter shots before moving on to full swings and full shots. I hit about thirty shots, not particularly aiming in any general direction to start with, or any specific distance. I will just be trying to swing rhythmically, thinking about my tempo. I don't put any pressure on myself before play, the only thing I am trying to achieve before play is preparing myself for the round of golf. After I have hit half swings with my wedge, I will then begin to hit full shots.

It is important to take your time, as if you try and hurry you probably end up swinging too quickly.

The next club I move on to is the 6 iron. My thinking is the same, and hopefully so is my tempo. I will hit twenty to thirty shots, not really worrying how they are going or in which direction. Once I feel my swing loosening up and the shots going well, I will change to a 4 iron, repeating the process. After the 4 I move on to a fairway wood, and only then to the driver.

When I start hitting the driver, I am not trying to see how far I can hit the ball, I concentrate on keeping my rhythm and tempo. I have fourteen clubs in the bag, not fourteen swings, and I will therefore try and change things as little as possible when I move from one club to another. After the driver I will hit a few more wedge or sand wedge shots, all the time concentrating on tempo.

You don't have to use the clubs I use, however you will find it helpful to start with a short iron, then hit a few mid irons, then long irons and woods.

PART TWO

CHAPTER 5

Tips from the Girls

One of the greatest things about golf is the people playing the game. I am fortunate to have some wonderful golfing friends all over the world. For the next chapter I have engaged the help of six very good friends. I have had the pleasure of knowing and watching them play golf, some of them for what seems years, others not so long. I hope you enjoy their tips as much as I have.

PENNY GRICE-WHITTAKER

I have played most of my amateur and professional golf at the same time as Penny. We played youth internationals together and were on England's gold medal winning team in the 1982 Junior European Team Championships. We played for England in the Home Internationals at the same time. However, I don't think I ever really got to know Penny until we went to play in Japan together. Along with Murial Thompson we had three hysterical weeks of laughter.

In 1991 she had a fairytale year winning two events, the first being the most prestigious event in women's professional golf, The Ladies British Open.

In winning the 1991 Weetabix British Open Penny became the first mother to do so. Penny has a little boy, and her tip is on how to play golf when pregnant.

 **PLAYING WHILST PREGNANT**

The advice that doctors have given pregnant women over the years has changed drastically. They seem to have gone from one extreme to the other. There was a time when they would tell you to sit and knit with your feet up for virtually all of your pregnancy. The modern idea, however, is that if you did it before you were pregnant, you can do it once you become pregnant. They

say that if you went jogging before you can jog whilst pregnant; if you played tennis, you can continue to play tennis; and if you played golf, continue to play golf.

Hearing their advice doesn't make things any easier though. We all want to do the best for our baby, and are obviously concerned that anything we may do will affect it.

My gynaecologist said that unless I was in pain and something wasn't right then I could 'play away', and I continued playing in professional tournaments until well into my pregnancy.

The last event I played in was at the beginning of August and I gave birth to Oliver on 7th October 1989. Looking back I am sure that playing so much golf helped to keep me in good shape, and as a result I had a very easy pregnancy. I had no back problems – obviously if I had had there would have been no way I could have continued playing golf. I have noticed other girls on tour who have had babies have all been able to stay playing for a long time. Maybe all the turning does us good.

The one tip I would give to pregnant women who want to play golf is: Don't change anything too much. I think there is a tendency that, because you have a big lump in front of you, you try and clear quickly to get it out of the way so that you can hit through to the target. I would say, don't fight it, slow down, just try and time it, let your body come through naturally. I actually swung more slowly, and hit the ball better. The only thing you might obviously change is your set-up position. Make sure at address that you are well balanced, because if you lean too far forward, when the baby begins to get bigger, you will actually fall forward.

JANE CONNACHAN

Jane started playing golf when she was four, and by the time she was eleven she had represented Scotland at full international level. At sixteen she became the youngest golfer ever to play for Great Britain.

I first met Jane when I was nineteen and playing in the Scottish Girls' Open Stroke Play Championship where we were paired together in the last round. Jane won that event, and continued winning top amateur tournaments, including the British stroke play, Scottish Championship, British Girls' (twice), Australian Girls', Scottish Girls' (three times). As a professional she has won five tournaments on the European tour, including the European Open.

Her tip is on the short game.

TIP 30 AIM AT THE TOP OF THE PIN

Too often when I am playing with amateurs their shots to the pin finish short. This is especially noticeable with 90-yard shots, which I would expect to get up to the pin. Most of the trouble on British courses is at the entrance to the greens. The front of the greens are often heavily bunkered, and if you don't get used to hitting the ball up to the pin, you will also be in danger of landing in the bunker, when the pin is placed at the front of the green.

If you watch the professionals play, you will notice that although they are not always on line, their ball will finish parallel to the hole. None of us will get the line right on every shot, but if your "off line" shots are pin high you will still have a chance of making the putt.

To help solve this problem try aiming for the top of the pin instead of the bottom. Don't be frightened to hit over the pin. Too many golfers seem to be frightened of the green and are timid in the way they attempt to play their shots. A bold, crisp shot is needed when you pitch. If you try and steer the ball or help it to the target you will only mis-hit the shot.

DIANE BARNARD

Diane has one of the most classical swings on the women's tour. If you want to see a strong graceful swing then I would advise a couple of hours watching her play. In 1990 Diane was rewarded for her hard work when she won the BMW Ladies

Classic and finished tenth in the order of merit. Since her win Diane has confirmed herself as one of the top English professionals on the Women's tour.

Diane's tip is on putting.

TIP 31 · BALLS UNDER YOUR ARMPITS

In a perfect putting stroke there should be no wrist action at all. The putting stroke should be controlled by the larger muscles in the top half of your body.

By placing a golf ball under each armpit during your practice, you will get the feeling of the pendulum action adopted by most top professionals, which gives a consistent and effective putting stroke.

During the putting stroke your arms should hang freely, without allowing your elbows to stick out excessively from the sides of your body. If your elbows stick out too much it will be difficult to promote the correct wrist and hand action, and your putting will be inconsistent under pressure. Similarly, if the arms and hands are held too tightly against your body, they will become too tense, resulting in a twitchy putting stroke. It is vital that the shoulders and arms are able to swing freely back and through in a firm but relaxed manner.

If you try the "ball under the armpit" drill, it has three benefits. Firstly, it does not allow you to hold your arms too closely to your body, as it will cause great discomfort. Secondly, if your elbows stick out excessively at address the balls will fall out from under your arms. Lastly, if you do not swing arms and shoulders in one piece, and let the arms race away in either the backswing or the follow through, one or other of the balls will fall out.

PEGGY REECE

Although not a professional, you can find no better example of someone playing top class golf for nearly 50 years than Peggy Reece. Born in 1920, she was Gloucestershire County Champion 10 times, and runner up 12 times. She won the South West Amateur 5 times and was runner up 8 times.

Maybe her best national finish was as finalist in the 1961 English Amateur, the year of my birth; 20 years later, still playing for the county, we played foursomes together for Gloucestershire. She has been both county and country selector, Chairman of the South West Division and England Captain.

Giving the appearance of a sweet old lady, an ideal granny, she is a tiger on the golf course.

I shall never forget my first British Amateur Championships. I had just lost to the no 1 seed, when I noticed the crowds heading off down to the third hole. They were going off to watch Peggy, tussling with Australia's no 1, Jane Lock. Few there could believe it when this little white haired lady in her 60s won at the 25th, 7 extra holes. Those of us from Gloucestershire were not in the least surprised. It has been a trademark of Peggy's golfing career to give it her best shot, regardless of who the opponent was.

When it comes to giving a tip on how to play golf for over 50 years there is none better than Peggy.

Her tips are as follows.

PLAY WELL FOR YEARS

When I left school I made a vow to keep fit, without being neurotic about it.

Playing golf is obviously a good way to keep trim; however, I do also think we need to keep fit for golf.

I've developed my "five essentials" for playing golf over the years.

1 Strong legs are essential for golf; skipping or running will make sure they stay firm and strong.

2 I always play a match as if it were a medal, disciplining myself to think only about my score and how I am doing in relation to par, not trying to beat my opponent. Nine times out of ten if I beat par I will beat my opponent.

3 Again, in competitions, try not to make the first mistake, concentrating on doing the simple things well; let others take the chances.

4 Preparation! I always get to the course well in advance of my tee time. Not only to warm up, but to prepare myself mentally, which to me is more important than hitting practice shots.

5 Don't spend too much time trying to get your swing right on your own, go to your professional, and use his swing as a mirror.

MEREDITH MARSHALL

Meredith is from Tampa, Florida, and since her first trip to the European Tour in 1983 she has become a regular visitor to the British Isles. Her best finish was in winning the Bowering Scottish Open. She combines playing the tour with teaching at the Yeovil Golf Club in Somerset.

It's not hard to imagine Meredith being good at any sport she tries. In fact she was East Coast surf champion before she started taking golf "seriously".

From her experience in teaching and playing different sports her tip is on preparation.

GET A ROUTINE

TIP 33

It has become apparent to me that when golfers get under pressure or in a tight situation they don't always pay attention to things that they would normally do when they are relaxed and thinking clearly; unless, that is, they have taught themselves a routine that they stick to whatever the circumstances.

If you have a routine, and practise it until it becomes second nature, you can programme a successful shot pattern into your memory bank, so that when you are nervous, you will not play your shot too quickly or without proper thought, but will still go through "the routine"

I have a routine I use on every shot to the green. You might find it helpful to try it, or make one up for yourself.

STEP 1 Decide which club to use.
STEP 2 Stand behind the ball and visualize the ball flying towards the target.
STEP 3 Whilst still standing behind the ball, line up with a piece of grass or mud a few inches in front of the ball on the ball-to-target line, and then come round and line up the leading edge of the club with the spot.

STEP 4 Grip club.
STEP 5 Feet together.
STEP 6 Left foot moves a couple of inches left, right foot moves to the right.
STEP 7 Check body is parallel to ball-to-target line.
STEP 8 Look at target once more.
STEP 9 Look at the ball and commence swing.

This is a simple routine and will improve consistency and concentration.

GILLIAN STEWART

Since her first year on the Women's Tour in 1985, Gillian has been one of the most professional and consistent players the tour has produced. During this time she has won two events and has had numerous top place finishes.

As an amateur, Gillian was equally successful winning the Scottish Women's Amateur three times, the Under-Nineteens, and the Girls' twice. She also won the British Girls' and represented Scotland and Great Britain on numerous occasions.

Her tip is on bunker play.

TIP 34

TEST THE SAND

It is not against the rules that, whilst taking your stance in a bunker, you feel what sort of sand is in it.

The rules of golf stipulate that you are not allowed to go into a bunker and test the sand to see whether it is hard or soft sand: they say you can't build a stance to help you hit the ball. However, Rule 13-3 allows a player to place her feet firmly in the bunker whilst taking her stance.

You can take full advantage of this rule when playing from a bunker. Most players like to wiggle their feet into the sand to secure a firm foothold, and in doing this you get a good idea of what the sand is like.

If your feet go through the sand easily it will show that the sand is light, and then when you swing down the club will move through the sand easily.

If when you step into the bunker it feels really hard, for instance after rain, then you know the sand will be harder to hit through.

Sometimes the sand may look soft, but upon stepping into the bunker, however, it becomes apparent that beneath the soft surface lies a hard interior. When you take your stance and wiggle your feet into the sand you will be able to tell, and still be within the rules.

Having this information will give you confidence either to hit the ball softly, as you should from soft sand, or to hit it with less sand as you would from hard sand.

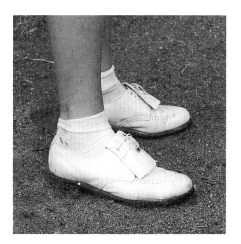

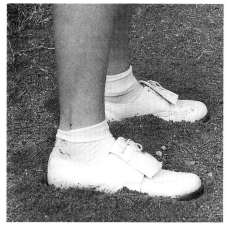

Wriggle your foot to see whether the sand is soft or hard

CHAPTER 6

Exercises for Golf

 **STRENGTHEN
YOUR ARMS**

For most women golfers it is their hands and arms which form the weakest link in their golf swings. When this is the case, the strong muscles in the body tend to take over in the swing.

This, for example, is one of the reasons your shoulders might pull across the ball, resulting in a top.

It is your hands and arms which need to be strong in order to hit the ball from the rough or out of tight lies.

Your arms need to be strong so that they will not collapse at the top of the swing and loose width, which will affect the distance you hit the ball.

By STRONG, I don't mean that you need to be a weight lifter or become muscle-bound. No, but you need to have a certain strength in your arms in order to swing cor-

rectly. You need to develop GOLF MUSCLES.

During the ladies' golf clinics, I often do a couple of little tests to show everyone how strong or weak they are. You might like to try this for yourselves.

Left arm test

First of all take any club in your left hand, address the ball as you would normally, except of course, that your right hand is not on the club.

Start your backswing in slow motion, turning your shoulders and hips as usual, although your left arm is not going to be aided by your right arm.

At the top of your swing, stop and hold the club still.

If your left arm is not very strong, you will find it difficult to hold the club still and will probably quickly have to lower your arm.

Most golfers have problems doing this correctly because the left arm is

not strong enough to support their swings. If you spend a few minutes three times a week swinging a club with your left arm you will soon strengthen it and build golf muscles which will help maintain your width at the top of your swing.

Do not try and keep your left arm

NOTE YOU ARE NOT JUST PICK-ING THE CLUB UP IN THE AIR WITH YOUR LEFT ARM, YOU MUST TAKE UP A PROPER STANCE, AND TURN YOUR SHOULDERS AS YOU WOULD IN YOUR SWING (SEE PHOTO). YOUR LEFT ARM MUST FOLLOW A PROPER SWING PATH FOR THIS EXERCISE TO BE BENEFICIAL.

rigid, firmly straight is correct. You don't have to go on to the driving range or even on to the golf course to do this, you can try it in your garden, garage or maybe even in the living room. It is one of the golf practices which, although easy and taking only a few minutes will really benefit your swing.

TIP 36   ## HIT WITH THE LEFT

We are now going to take the one-arm swing a step further.

Once you are able to swing the golf club with only one hand and arm, try the drill and stop at the top of your swing for a few seconds, holding the club very steady. After you have tried this for a few weeks you are ready to try to hit shots with your left arm.

It does become easy to just swing the club with the left arm, it is not so easy to try to co-ordinate your left arm and try to hit a ball. It is not an exaggeration to say nearly everyone misses the first time they try to hit balls left-handed. However, it is worth persevering as it is really useful for strengthening and co-ordination. It is one drill that you will see top professionals using on the practice ground. If you have trouble making contact with the ball, start by taking the club back only a few inches; then as you begin to get a feel for hitting with one arm, take a slightly longer swing. Continue extending the short swing until you have reached a full backswing. To begin with, don't try and hit too hard.

The idea is to strengthen your left arm so that it will work correctly in your swing; if you swing too quickly you will not swing correctly. If you try and hit too hard it will probably result in your stronger muscles taking over.

You don't want to spend hours doing this, I would recommend hitting ten balls normally with both hands on the club, then ten left-hand only shots and so on through your practice balls.

Remember, nothing happens overnight; but if you start now, in a few weeks' time you will certainly notice a difference.

STRENGTHEN BOTH ARMS

The second thing I try at clinics is as follows, and it's amazing to see how even strong men find it difficult.

Take a club in your left hand. Turn it upside down, and hold the bottom of the shaft around the hosel. Straighten your arm, holding your hand at shoulder height.

Try moving the club through your fingers towards the other end of the club eventually reaching the grip end.

Most people find it difficult to co-ordinate their fingers whilst holding the club and trying to move it in an upward direction. It also becomes heavier the further you work down the shaft, and progressing to the grip might be impossible at first.

This drill is like many others, becomes easier the more often you do it. Therefore, when you can do it once try twice, gradually building

up the number of times you can do it. You can also try this with your right hand. I have done the drill with both hands at the same time. However, most of the time I will try it five times with the right and then five with the left. This is another of the drills which can be done anywhere, you don't have to go to the golf club to improve your golf.

SWING A HEAVY CLUB

All golfers who want to improve their game are faced with the same problem: where to start.

Experience has taught me that unless you are fairly fit and strong you will find it difficult to achieve the correct backswing position. For this reason the obvious place to start is with your "golf muscles". There doesn't seem to be anything quite like hitting balls and swinging a club to help strengthen the muscles you use in the swing.

On my first trip to Florida in 1982 I became friendly with a 65-year-old professional, John McMeeking, who had lived in America for about forty years but was originally from Scotland. He had a special club that he had made himself. It had the biggest head on it I had ever seen and he had drilled additional holes in the sole and filled them with lead. He gave it to me to swing a few times. I found it very difficult to start with as my hands were not strong enough to control it very well. I had no problem swinging through, since it was so heavy it used to go through all on its own. I started swinging this club for a short time every day, and found that it really helped me swing the club solidly and improved my strength.

With a heavy club I had to swing slowly and so I could feel every part of my swing, which made it easier to concentrate on turning my body, keeping width and not having too long a swing.

I would also practise going to the top of my backswing and holding the club there for a few seconds.

Before leaving Florida John gave me that club, and it has lasted well over the past ten years. I don't take it with me to tournaments, but during the winter, especially if I'm not playing every day, I have a few minutes swinging my heavy club, which keeps my muscles from losing strength.

If you have an old wooden club, it is a very simple thing to get your professional to take the sole plate off and add extra weight. Alternatively there are now weights on sale which slip over the grip of your club, slide down the shaft and are easily attached at the neck. It is also useful to swing two clubs, where you place one head of the club on top of the

other and hold both grips in your hands and swing.

How heavy a club you swing will depend on how strong you are and how long you have been playing. If you are a beginner, simply swinging a light club is difficult, so wait a couple of months before going on to something heavier. When you do start using a heavy club just try quarter swings, taking the club back very slowly and through slowly, then gradually build up to half, then three-quarter swings. If you have been playing quite a while and are fairly strong then experiment to see how heavy a club you can use.

This is a great practice for the back garden.

TIP 39 — STAYING POWER AND STAMINA

You can't be as dogmatic in a statement about who can and who can't play golf as you in other sports. For instance, you don't see very overweight sprinters, tennis and squash players. You don't see pro athletes drinking and smoking in the bar after a meet in the same way golfers do. The sausage sandwiches that have become a tradition during the annual Sunningdale foursomes competition would be frowned upon in many other sports. So, does it matter?

There have been fat winners

of tournaments, little skinny winners, smokers, non-smokers, all-night-partiers and early-to-beds! However, I cannot see any who don't take care of their bodies lasting as long as those who do. Gary Player is an example to us all: still incredibly fit, playing good golf and far outlasting most of his contemporaries.

If you are physically 'fit' there is no doubt that everything your body does, from walking upstairs to shopping during the sales, will be easier than for a person who is not fit. Fitness is not whether you can or cannot do something, but rather, after the activity, how quickly you recover. It doesn't matter if you take three minutes to recover after walking up a flight of stairs, but if you walk up a hill on the golf course and cannot supply enough strength and co-ordination to execute an evenly timed shot, you are not going to do very well.

It is interesting to note that during the winter I do a lot of stamina training, and in the past four years I have won three tournaments in sudden-death extra hole play offs. At the Tytherington club during the English Open, I had to play three extra holes before eventually winning. I do not think it was solely my physical fitness that enabled me to win, but it certainly played an important part. Mentally and physically, I had staying power.

When I first started to play golf, my father stressed the importance of being physically fit, not only for golf, but also for travelling. Anyone who follows either the men's or women's tour will know the sort of crazy travel routine we can have. We travel to different countries, having to perform when we arrive; there is no time for jet-lag. It's not like going on holiday, where you can relax after long flights or delays, etc.

If you decide to do some training, it should include strengthening, aerobic and stretching exercises. Joining a gym is the best and safest way to start. Most good gyms would be able to advise you on what to attempt for your age and aspirations. Although I would think that it is the youngsters who are more likely to take up this tip, it applies to all age groups. Keeping your limbs lithe and supple for the future has to start today!

 **JUNIORS**

The biggest problem most juniors face is that they have young undeveloped bones and muscles, and are therefore not very strong. Indeed, the children who develop physically first often head the leader boards in junior competitions. This need not put smaller children off, as given time they usually catch up, and often surpass the child prodigies.

It is important for younger golfers, especially those who develop a love for the game and tend to spend all their holidays playing golf, to do contra exercises. By that I mean exercises to counter the effect that playing golf has on the body.

Think about your fingers, wrapped tightly round the grip whilst putting for hours; then your stance, bent over, shoulders squeezed together. It can't be good for your posture, whatever your age, although youngsters will obviously be more affected.

The best exercise I know for fingers is probably playing the piano. However, it's not everyone that has access to a piano. Stretching your fingers will be helpful. Press your finger tips together whilst your palms are slightly apart.

For keeping shoulders supple first lie on the ground, stomach down, with your hands against the ground under your shoulders. Push up slightly, keeping your hips on the ground. Then, staying in the same position, put your arms out along the ground above your head and slowly lift your arms from the ground. If you are able to do this easily, hold a stick in your hands and lift the stick. Stand with your back against a wall, and bend both arms with your wrists against the wall next to your shoulders; this will pull your shoulders back.

I think most adults, although knowing that these exercises would do them good, would have a hard time remembering to do them, but if you can impress their importance upon young golfers, in time they will thank you.

CHAPTER 7

Practice

 **TIP 41**

HOW TO PRACTISE

Have you heard the saying, 'practice makes perfect'? I would like to change it slightly and say that

PERFECT PRACTICE MAKES PERFECT

It is the "**HOW**" that is important when practising, not just hitting balls at the range. I remember a young rookie professional saying after reviewing the year that she was going to work really hard on her short game through the winter. Another experienced player, Peggy Conley, asked her "How?"; unfortunately, she had no idea!

Some golfers I know don't want to use the practice range because they say it's boring or they play worse after practising. Aimless practice is boring, and you probably will feel you are playing worse afterwards. When you go on to the practice ground, you should always have a goal or a purpose for going there. Don't just go and aimlessly hit balls.

Over the years I have seen many golfers practising hard, yet they don't seem to make any headway. Simply spending two hours on the range every day will not necessarily benefit your golf. YES, you'll probably get blisters and become a little stronger, but you could well be grooving some swing faults which will take a long time to eradicate.

How and what you practise will govern how quickly you improve. If you spend time doing the right sort of practice you will reap the rewards of your labour. In understanding it is the 'HOW' that is important, I divide my practice into four categories.

CATEGORY 1	**CATEGORY 2**
Technique	Developing feel

CATEGORY 3	**CATEGORY 4**
Pressure practice	Strength and co-ordination

CATEGORY 1: TECHNIQUE

The first thing all golfers should work on during practice is their technique. By this I mean the method which you use to swing the golf club. It is worth bearing in mind that the only reason for making a swing is to move the ball from where it is to where you want it to finish.

The easiest way is the simplest, and the simplest is the method which will repeat, time after time, and especially under pressure.

There are obviously many ways to swing a golf club, and golfers with a variety of swings have won big tournaments, even so it is usually the technically correct which last over many years. For this reason, there are certain BASICS which would commonly be taught by nearly every PGA professional.

Whatever the proficiency of your play it is always possible to improve your technique. The easiest way to do this is obviously with a professional. After discussing your faults, you should decide the order in which you are going to tackle them, and write them down to remind yourself of what you are working on.

 **TIP 42** **THE BEGINNER**

If you are about to start playing golf take lessons from a qualified profes-

sional. It is definitely the easiest way to start.

After the first lesson, a beginner should practise how to hold the club correctly. You don't need to go to the golf course to do this. Have a few clubs positioned around the house, in the kitchen, lounge or even in the broom cupboard, so that when you get your vacuum cleaner out, there is your club. Pick it up, and try holding it with the correct grip, give it a few waggles, and then put it down. If you do this sort of thing a few times a day it will really help you progress quickly.

Remember, a little practice and often is better than a lot and seldom!

Once The Grip is mastered work on how to align the clubface and your body. It will help to do some strengthening and co-ordination exercises immediately you start golf. However there is no point in trying categories two and three until you have a good idea how to swing the club.

After a lesson you should go out and try to hit thirty balls, remembering what you have been told to do in the last lesson. This should always be done to reinforce what you have been taught during the lesson and will help you work out in your own mind exactly what you should be doing. If you are not sure about anything, go back and ask your professional to run through the technique again.

THE INTERMEDIATE AND ADVANCED

Don't ever think that to want to improve you must be a fanatic, or practise every day. **The better your technique, in fact, the less you will have to practise to maintain your game.**

Getting the most from anything you do really means attention to detail. If you enjoy cooking, you'll love scouring recipe books; if you enjoy photography, you will read and try camera techniques; and it's the same with golf. You will enjoy it more, the better you perform, even if you play only for fun and don't want a handicap or to play in competitions.

A video camera is an excellent teaching aid, firstly to pinpoint swing faults, and secondly to convince us of them. Often, when we are told something we don't believe it; however, if the evidence is shown on a television screen we can't doubt.

Once you have decided what needs working on, it's on to the range. Try to divide your balls into groups of ten. After hitting each group, evaluate how they are going. You don't want to spend the whole

practice session working on your technique, divide it between the different areas of your game that you need to work on. Make sure you leave at least half your time for short game and putting.

Remember to concentrate on one area of your technique at a time. Don't attempt to put all your faults right at once. Take your time, otherwise things will get missed or only half done. If you are changing something in your swing don't worry too much what is happening to the ball – you should be paying attention to the swing.

If you are an intermediate or advanced player you are going to be playing quite a lot, which will make it difficult to work on faults in your game.

For this reason the best time to work on changes to your swing is after the playing season, or before it starts.

If you are playing whilst making major changes, don't expect to play well. It is a case of two steps forward, one step back. When you are playing try not to think too much about your swing, but think instead of how and where you want the ball to go.

CATEGORY 2: DEVELOPING FEEL

When applied to golf, feel is an instinctive aptitude, an awareness by touch, which can be developed like many other skills. The ease with which you progress will vary from one player to another.

The beginner

Once you have an idea about the basics – Grip, Aim, Stance, Take-away, etc. – it's time to start working on your feel. It is important that you start to develop your feel when you practise and not spend all your time working on technique. For most beginners there is very little difference in distance between clubs, i.e. the 6 iron and the 4 iron will go roughly the same distance. Fear not, this will change the more you play golf and the stronger your golfing muscles become.

The intermediate and advanced

The more proficient you become at golf, the more important it will be for you to have good feel. You need to be able to feel what is happening in your swing so that if things go wrong you can put them right. Or if you want to hit an unusual shot, i.e. punching a 4 iron out from under trees so that it goes the distance of a 7 iron but keeps low under overhanging branches.

THE SHORT GAME

Developing feel in the short irons is very similar to feel in the long irons. There is no set club for any shot. What influences which club and shot to play is

1 **HOW THE BALL IS LYING**
2 **WHAT IS BETWEEN YOU AND THE HOLE**
3 **HOW QUICKLY THE BALL HAS TO STOP**
4 **WHERE THE PIN IS ON THE GREEN**
5 **HOW CONFIDENT YOU ARE IN PLAYING THE SHOT**

These five factors need to be brought into your practice session so that you can develop a feel for how to play shots in different circumstances and from various distances, whether the ball is in long grass, a tight lie, muddy ground or even a gravel path. It can be fun experimenting.

Around the chipping green at Long Ashton we have all these conditions and I take every opportunity to try them all. I rarely finish on a gravel path, where there is no provision in the local rules for dropping the ball. However, during practice I will hit a few from this position there so that I know how to play the shot should I ever have to. When

members see me hitting from the gravel in practice they must think it rather strange, but I remember having to play what seemed an impossible shot from a gravel path in a Tournament at Calcot Park, and was able to make par. Make a point to practise from all conditions, not just the perfect lies.

Try every club, don't be frightened to have a chip IN PRACTICE, with your 3 iron. It is good practice to take fifty balls to the edge of the green and hit ten each with the wedge, 9, 8, 7 and 6 iron. Pick them up and try it again with the 5, 4 and 3 iron. Try playing the 4 iron from where you need the sand wedge. All these things will really develop a feel for what it will take to get the ball near the hole, and so when you do miss the green you have a variety of shots to choose from.

TIP 45 DEVELOPING FEEL FOR THE LONG GAME

One of my most memorable shots in 1991 was at the Tytherington Club during the English Open. The eighth hole is a very interesting par 4. The tee shot is played towards a small 40-yard opening in the trees and there are lateral hazards, in the trees on the left and in the trees on the right. It has a small green, well bunkered, with what looks like an elephant buried in the middle of it, by that I mean a big hump.

Most players hit iron off the tee so that they will not go near the trees or

hazards. I hit driver on two days because it was into the wind, and I didn't want to leave myself a tricky shot into the green.

In the third round, I hit a slight hook with my driver, which after a couple of bad bounces left the ball hanging over the edge of the hazard and under the trees. I was only about 110 yards from the pin and yet the nearest I could aim to the flag was fifty yards right. I therefore took my 7 iron and hit an easy shot with a closed club face which started out 50 yards right of the green and hooked back on to the middle of the putting surface. I made a par 4 out of what could have been a 6 or 7 and went on to win the tournament.

If I had not tried this in practice, I wouldn't have known the difference in feel between a 7 iron going 100 yards and 140 yards, or the difference between that same shot going high or low, left or right.

To develop a feel for playing shots different distances put an umbrella in the ground about 100 yards away and try to hit every iron in the bag to it. Then place it at 130 yards and try doing the same. Try hitting a draw, starting the shot to the right of the target and then a fade, starting left of the target. Both shots should finish on line.

Practice shots from different circumstances

CATEGORY 3: GET A GOAL

TIP 46

It is said of Gary Player that he wouldn't leave his bunker practice until he had holed several balls in a row. No wonder he is the best bunker player in the world.

If you want to be a top class golfer you have to go to these extremes and there are no short cuts, it is all hard work. There is no substitute for practice, but for the average golfer a goal of holing one ball from the bunker before going home might be impossible. However, setting goals and putting pressure on ourselves is a must if we want to perform when we play on the course.

If you have high hopes for your golf then the sooner you start recognizing this the better, although this doesn't excuse those golfers who don't have lofty expectations for their golf. If you want to enjoy your golf, the best way is by improving your play. Perhaps the beginner should not leave the bunker until every shot had been hit out of it. The slightly better player has to hit the green with ten shots in a row.

Once these goals are easily accomplished the ten shots have to be at least 10 feet from the pin, then 5 feet, then within a dustbin lid, and so on.

The same sort of pressure can be applied to chipping, starting with an

easy target and increasing the difficulty as you increase your skill.

With the longer irons, hit to a practice green if possible. If not put something out to aim for, an umbrella or bucket. Low handicap players should try hitting twenty balls, every one of which must finish on the green. If one ball misses you have to hit them all over again. Do this with any iron up to about a 5 iron, though with the 5 iron you might allow yourself one shot missing the green. For higher handicappers set yourself an easier goal, i.e. hitting the green with half the shots with your 8 iron. A beginner might try to hit the green with two balls out of twenty with the 8 iron.

When practising in this way, use the same tactic as in pressure putting. With the last few balls think of something you would like to achieve, perhaps cutting your handicap and having to carry the water to reach the green to achieve it; or maybe hitting a good tee shot on your "bogey" hole. Depending on your handicap, assimilate in your mind what you would have to do to reach your goal. Then say to yourself, 'If I make par here I will win, so the better and closer I hit the ball to the pin the easier it will be to make par.'

It is amazing how tense you can become in a practice situation, especially if you miss the green a few times and have to start again, but this is what we want, and by sticking with it, persevering, you will be able to perform when it really does matter.

CATEGORY 4: STRENGTH AND CO-ORDINATION

 **PUTT FOR THE TROPHY**

With any practice it is important not to be aimless and just hit balls, and this is no less important on the putting green, whether it is putting before you go out to play or spending time working on your technique.

Whatever your standard, you can put pressure on yourself by playing games or setting goals. The reason we want to put pressure on ourselves is that during competitions a high proportion of golfers play worse than when they are not in a competitive situation. Nervousness and tension often lead to a lower performance.

If we develop skills during practice which makes us feel as we would during a tournament, we learn to overcome nervousness and tension, negative thoughts and feelings.

Stand six feet from the hole with six balls. For the beginner, stand a little closer to start with, then, as you improve, move back. Keep putting until you hole all six in a row. When you get to the last couple of balls, say to yourself, "This

one is to make birdie at the seventeenth, and I'm in the lead of the monthly medal" (or club championship, county championship, British Open, whatever your aspirations might be). Even if it's only to beat your husband, or best friend or to cut your handicap, make holing that ball really important. If you hole the fifth ball then the last putt is to win the match or the trophy.

When I started playing golf I practised this drill nearly every day. I used to say the sixth putt was to win the British Amateur in a sudden-death play off. In the semi-final of the 1982 British Amateur Championship at Walton Heath, on the nineteenth hole I had a six-foot putt to beat Mary McKenna, and thereby proceeded to the final. I made that putt and went on to win the most prestigious tournament in women's amateur golf, The British Amateur Championship, which had been my goal since starting to play golf. I sincerely believe that the way I had practised made it possible for me to deal with the nerves and tension I had when I stood over that putt.

If you make yourself concentrate, and put yourself in a pressure situation whilst practising, when you come to the real thing you will have more confidence to achieve your goal. You can say to yourself, 'I have done this before, and I can do it now!'

Of course I still miss putts, everyone misses putts now and then. However, the reason will not be that I am nervous of the situation, but more likely that I read the putt incorrectly.

TIP 48 — MULTIPLE HITS

Often at the beginning of a season my muscles don't feel as firm and strong as they were at the end of the previous golfing season. What I have found helps bring back form and that good feeling of strong hands is hitting one shot after another in quick succession, without stopping to regrip the club or change stance.

I line up ten balls four inches or so apart then address the first ball and hit it. At the completion of my follow through I don't address the next ball, I simply swing from the top of the first follow through, straight to my backswing, whilst moving my feet a little closer to the next ball so that I don't have to reach too far forward. I then swing straight down to hit the second ball, continuing like this until all ten balls have been hit. Sometimes I will do this fairly slowly for co-ordination, at other times as quickly as I can, which really strengthens hands and forearms.

If you are going to try this I would suggest you put the balls further away from each other than four inches, because if you put them too close together you might hit several balls at the same time. You might also find it easier to start with four balls in a row, and when your co-ordination and strength get better build up to ten.

I like hitting ten in a row like this, then ten with my left arm, then ten with both hands. This is an ideal way of dividing your balls in a practice session and will ensure you keep your interest.

FEET TOGETHER

I know we professionals must look very funny on the practice ground, sometimes all trying different drills, some with elastic straps across their chests, others with footballs between their knees and so on. 'Is all this really necessary?' you may ask. Some drills I would have to question as I have seen some very funny things, but there are plenty of good drills which can really help your game.

One such drill is hitting the ball with your feet together, and there are two reasons:

1 It strengthens your hands and arms
2 It shortens your swing

I would advise you to practise this with a 6 iron. Stand with your feet touching, then swing back as far as you can easily, making sure you keep your balance.

This is especially good for women golfers as we do not normally have strong hands and arms, which can result in a very weak, sloppy hit at impact. Practising with your feet together will help you use your hands.

Practising with your feet together will also restrict your swing, because if you swing back too far you will lose balance. As most women have a tendency to swing back too far this drill will help as it promotes a shorter swing, making it easier to produce the power where it is needed: at the ball.

I would also try this with my driver during a practice session. Most golfers feel the need to HIT the driver harder, but what normally happens is that they mis-hit it harder. By swinging with the driver with your feet together you will learn to time the ball better, and if you swing too long or your shoulders move forward you will fall over.

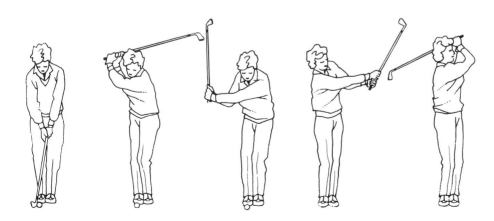

VARY YOUR SHOTS

No matter how varied your practice, it is still easy to lose concentration and become bored. The more games you invent, the more you will enjoy practising.

Mastering draws, hooks, fades, slices, high and low shots will keep your concentration and help your feel and control.

We have already discussed briefly (chapter 2) how your swing and the direction the clubface is aiming affect the way the ball will fly.

Some players change their grips to effect a change in the direction the ball will go. I find it easier, if I want the ball to draw or fade, etc., to change my alignment, and then open or close the clubface unless, for instance, a severely hooked shot is required, and then I would swing on an in-to-out plane as well.

The swing geometry might seem complicated to the beginner, but it is essential you understand what is going on, even if you are not yet able to do anything about it. Learning how to change the direction in which the ball flies is a must for the better player.

Try experimenting with body alignment, change the direction the clubface is aiming at address and the path the club takes in your backswing, see how these swing changes affect the direction of the ball.

With this knowledge, you can make the ball go in the direction you want it to go. However, learning to control the ball so that you hit the shot "WHEN" you want will take time.

During practice, put a target out at about 140 yards. Then experiment, hitting every kind of shot to the target – high fades, low draws, etc. Once you can hit them all, and know how to change your address position, etc., to hit each shot, try hitting them to order, and give yourself a mark for how near the target they finish. Have a competition with a friend to help to hone this skill under pressure. You can take it in turns naming the shot you should hit, and provided it is the correct shape, nearest the pin wins.

Practising this way can turn your dreary practice into.a most rewarding time, and it can be fun!

 **LOOK INTO THE MIRROR**

Mirror, mirror on the wall told the wicked old queen who was 'the fairest of them all', and it can tell you a thing or two as well.

I have learnt to use mirrors, patio doors, even large windows, to view my swing.

Set up

The first thing to check in the mirror is your set up. Are you too crouched? Do you look comfortable? Are your knees flexed? Is your back straight? Is your chin away from your shoulders? Are your hands and arms the correct distance from your body? Are your feet too far apart or too close together? These are all things you can easily see for yourself, without needing to have a lesson.

Look at your swing

The next thing to do, if you have enough room (watch the ceiling lights!) is view your swing. Look at how you start the club back. What are your shoulders, hips, legs, wrists and arms doing in your backswing? Where are your arms and hands at the top of your swing? Is your left arm very bent or too stiff? No matter what your standard, a lot can be learnt by looking, and you don't have to spend hours doing it, just five minutes from time to time.

If you are not quite sure about something in your set up or swing, this is the time to ask your professional for his or her advice. If you keep checking back you will soon know how you should look, then if things are not going right on the golf course the fault is much easier to correct.

TIP 52 — VARY THE DISTANCE

I often see golfers hitting all their practice balls from the same place when practising chipping. This might be useful for technique, but staying in the same place does little for your judgement, feel or visualization.

When I practise chipping I like to vary the distance, hitting no more than five or ten balls from each spot. I can do this one of two ways: either I change position and aim at the same flag, or I stay in the same place and aim at different targets. Either way will achieve the same objective. All good wedge players have good feel and visualization, they see what they want to happen to the ball before they hit it. If you practise in this way, you will develop much more feel, which will help turn those three shots into two.

TIP 53 — PLAY A ROUND IN YOUR HEAD

Before you play in a competition it is important that you prepare yourself mentally as well as physically. It is important for players of all standards to make sure that they are thinking positively as well as swinging correctly.

The mind, however, is probably that part of the game of golf neglected by your teacher or coach, mainly because their understanding of the mind is not on a par with their understanding of the swing.

This is understandable, the mind is generally a little understood subject, yet it is very powerful. A whole book could be devoted to the subject of your mind and how it affects your golf.

The first thing to acknowledge in this area is that how you think and feel will affect everything you do. To take this a step further, how you are thinking about your golf, and feel about your swing, will affect how you play.

Some players are very negative about their golf. If you keep on telling yourself you can't do something, there is a good chance that you won't. Then there are those players who are so positive about their golf that they falter because of overconfidence. If you think you can do it all there is a tendency to lose concentration.

Before you play it is important to be relaxed, but not too relaxed, keyed up but not too tense. The balance is controlled by your mind.

Imagery is an important sporting technique and is used by many top competitors in sports such as skiing, bob sleigh, motor racing even football, and it can be used in golf. Dale Reid, who has won more tournaments than any other player on the European Tour, plays the round of golf in her mind before play each day. Whilst other golfers are spending most of their time on the range, she sits quietly and thinks of each shot she is going to play, where it should finish, how she would attempt to hit it and so on.

Picturing your swing in your mind will help muscle memory and confidence.

Try to visualize yourself hitting good shots. Once you are able to do that, try playing a hole, and as this becomes easier play the whole golf course in your mind.

If you try this tip, you are not guaranteed to play the course as you did in your mind, but you will certainly stand a better chance.

PART THREE

CHAPTER 8

Putting

I have been told, over the years, that I am a good putter. This hasn't happened overnight. I have worked very hard and spent hours honing my technique and feel to make me into a good putter. During tournaments I like to putt for about three hours a day.

There are several characteristics that most good putters have in common.

1 They hold the putter so that their hands work together.
2 Their hands move back and through to the hole smoothly.
3 The ball comes off the putter face so that it hugs the ground, not jumping up in the air.

 **THE GRIP**

There are probably more differences in the putting grip than in any other part of the golf set up and swing. It might also be said that there are as many putting strokes as there are golfers. It is the one part of the game where professionals are not dogmatic about the exact way of holding the club. What I always tend to say with putting is, 'If it works, use it'! By that I mean, if you are a very good putter, you hole a lot of putts, then keep your putting stroke as it is. However, if you miss a lot of putts you think you should hole, or you would like to hole more putts, then (1) look at your technique to see if it needs changing, and (2) work on grooving a smooth consistent strike.

We have already established the importance of a good grip in the swing – if you don't grip the club correctly you can't swing correctly. This is not so true in the putting stroke, as there are a variety of ways to hold the putter and still achieve what is necessary in the putting stroke.

There are several important criteria when deciding how you want to hold the putter.

1 If the grip is easy to achieve it will be easy to repeat, whereas a complicated grip can be difficult to repeat.
2 The putter must be held so that your hands and arms can work together and move back from and through to the hole.
3 The putter should be gripped so that you have control of it.

I don't use the grip that I use for the rest of my clubs; I put my left hand index finger over the fingers of my right hand pointing down the shaft. The less you break your wrists, the more likely you are to putt consistently, and I have found that by having my left finger down the shaft it keeps my wrists firm. I take a fairly upright stance and have my hands and arms just hanging from my shoulders before gripping the club. I advocate a slightly wider stance than normal, for with too narrow a stance there is a tendency to sway, instead of standing firm.

FOLLOW THROUGH TO THE HOLE

TIP 55

It is obvious that the putter head should follow the ball towards the hole after the ball has been struck. The length at which it follows this line will vary depending on how long the putt is. What you don't want is an exaggerated follow-through. On the other hand, no follow-through at all will probably result in a jerky putting stroke, and a follow-through which goes through to the left or right of the hole will probably mean that the ball has gone in that direction. One of the most common causes of missed short putts is that the putting stroke doesn't go through to the target.

In your follow-through, it is important to remember that it is not your wrists which break taking the putter head to the target, neither do your arms just move on their own; your shoulders, arms and hands all move together. The shoulders obviously will only move a little, and they don't turn as they would in the swing, the movement with the shoulders is more like a rock.

A good ten-minute practice to check that your putting stroke is going to the target is this:

Stand a foot from the hole with six balls. Set up as you would normally, then without taking a backstroke, use your shoulders, arms and hands as you would in the follow-through and push the putter head towards the hole, rolling the ball into the centre. When you move the putter head forward make sure that you don't scoop the ball forward by hingeing your wrists.

Practising this drill will encourage muscle memory by grooving a stroke which goes to the hole. I wouldn't suggest that you do this for too long, ten minutes is long enough if you are practising other things, or five minutes before you go out to play. Do not attempt this any further from the hole as you will have to move your follow-through too quickly to get the ball to go to the hole.

> DO NOT TRY PUTTING LIKE THIS ON THE COURSE, AS THIS IS A PRACTICE DRILL ONLY AND IS AN ILLEGAL WAY OF HITTING THE BALL.

TIP 56 FEEL

We often rely on our eyes so much that it can stop us from developing feel. Developing a feel for how hard to hit the ball on the putting green is of primary importance if we ever want to get the ball into the hole, or if not in, very close.

Most beginners rely totally on their eyes to judge whether the ball was short, long, left or right. If you only use your eyes you are not encouraging a feel for where you hit the ball. If you can't differentiate between the shot that's gone a long way past and one that is too short, it will make it very difficult to know how hard to hit the ball.

I sometimes putt with my eyes closed in order to develop feel.

When we close our eyes, our other senses become more aware.

Stand ten feet from the hole with six balls and aim as you would normally with the first ball, but before hitting it towards the hole, close your eyes. Now hit the ball. Without looking up to see where the ball has gone, think about how your muscles moved, which ones you used, how hard you hit the ball. Where do you think the ball went? Once you've decided where the ball has gone, based on the feeling you had from your hands, open your eyes to see if you were right. Try the next ball doing the same.

If your balls are finishing to the right all the time or to the left, see if you can FEEL why. If they are mostly short, on the next putt try to hit a little harder than you did before. When you have hit the next shot, feel where it has finished then look to see if you were right.

Drills like this don't need to be done for hours, or even every day. The beginner will find it more helpful than will the more experienced golfer. But whatever your standard, you will find this a useful drill.

TIP 57 LINE UP AND FOLLOW THROUGH

It is important with any part of your swing and putting stroke that the clubhead goes back and through along the right lines. It becomes more important on the putting green than on the fairway, as the margin for error is less. When you are on the fairway the green you are aiming at can be thirty yards wide, whereas on the putting green, you are aiming at a hole 4¼ inches wide.

Periodically throughout the year make an effort to check that you are lined up correctly and are taking the putter back and through 'square' to the hole.

This can be done very successfully by putting two clubs on the ground either side of the hole, where they will act firstly as a check for your body alignment. Make sure that your feet, hips and shoulders are all on line, parallel with the club nearest to your feet.

Secondly, the clubs will show whether you are taking the putter back and through on line. Leave an inch either side of the putter head between the two clubs. Then hit a few putts.

Notice when you take the club back if the putter head hits either of the clubs on the ground, or goes closer to one of them on either the back or through stroke. If it hits either club it will mean that the putter head is not going back and through straight.

Put 2 clubs on the ground to check alignment and swing path

This should only be attempted within a club length of the hole, as from this distance it is fairly easy to make sure that you are properly lined up. From this distance, you take the club back straight from the ball and follow through straight to the target. On longer putts, your back stroke will go slightly inside the ball-to-target line on the backswing and should go closer to the club nearest your feet.

By practising this regularly, you will encourage a good set-up and a good foundation to the putting stroke.

TIP 58 — REGAINING YOUR CONFIDENCE

Beginners usually find putting the easiest part of the game. The better player you become, the more you realize the importance of having a good putting stroke and preserving it!

Playing in wind or rain, and constantly having to adjust to the speed of different greens affects not only the putting stroke but often confidence.

No matter how good a putter you are, there are times when you misjudge the speed of a green or the break of a putt, and in bad weather lose the firm bold strike necessary in good putting, which can result in a loss of confidence and feel. It is then difficult to get out of the never-ending chain: you have no confidence so you don't hit the putt well, and you can't hit the putt well because you've no confidence.

When I feel I'm not putting well I like to revert to a drill which takes my mind off the technique and re-

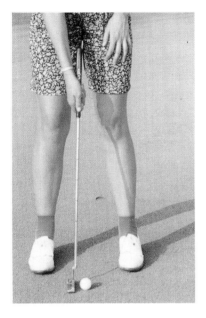

stores a good firm strike with feel. It is very easy to do, and within a short time I feel an improvement.

I firstly take my putter in my right hand, gripping it as I would normally for putting, then without placing my left hand on the club, I hit six putts to a hole about eight feet away. I make sure I am moving my hand and arm as I would normally when there are two hands on the putter. Next I hold the putter in my left hand only and repeat the six putts to the hole. Then having putted with both right and left hands I putt with both hands. I usually putt like this for ten to fifteen minutes, and find this helps me hit the putts firmly and with more confidence.

TIP 59 LONG PUTTING

It is difficult to line up with the green when you are 150 yards away, and it is equally difficult to aim correctly on the putting green or from the fringe when you are a long way from the hole.

Many golfers find it difficult to stand comfortably and tend to stand 'closed', aiming right of the target, which on a long putt has disastrous effects. It will mean that either the putt will go right or that you will try moving your whole body round to get the putter back on line, which normally results in a mis-hit putt. If you don't aim correctly on a long putt it will make it impossible to strike the ball with a smooth putting stroke, which is a must with long putts.

There are two things I think about when putting from long distances on or from the edge of the green.

The first thing to think about is to aim slightly left of the hole. If you think for a minute of a full swing, when you start your follow-through your hips and body are turning out of the way so that you can swing through to the target easily. In chipping, you stand with your feet slightly open because you do not have time in a short shot to move your hips and body out of the way. In either of these two swings, if your body doesn't get out of the way, it will be difficult to strike the ball squarely.

It is the same with long putts; you are taking the putter back a long way without using your body, and it is very easy to pull across your body in the follow-through because the ball has to go a long way. In aiming very slightly left on a long putt I get a better view of the line, and where I want the ball to go, and by aiming slightly left it's easier to hit the ball on the right line.

The second reason for standing slightly open is that it is easier for my shoulders, hands and arms to move together in one piece and to keep a good rhythm. I have found that on long putts if I stand on line my legs and hips want to move out of the

way and I therefore find it difficult to swing smoothly through the strike.

On long putts it is very important to keep the putter head accelerating through the ball, and if I stand on line I have found it restricts my follow-through, often resulting in a decelerated stroke a or mis-hit putt.

> I WOULD STRESS THAT THE STANCE IS ONLY OPEN HERE A FRACTION. DON'T TAKE THIS TIP TO AN EXTREME AND AIM 10 YARDS LEFT.

TIP 60   TAKE CARE NOT TIME

One of the things which makes golf such a fascinating game is that, unlike football pitches, tennis courts, squash courts or snooker tables, every golf course is different. Each hole and its green are different from all the others. Beginners obviously find this more of a problem than do better players. Learning to adjust parts of your game, and in particular putting, from course to course will only come with practice. Whatever your standard, you must take time to look at the green and judge the borrow and pace.

It is very rare to find a putt that is straight, especially the further you go from the hole. A large percentage of putts are on uneven ground, and therefore there must be some borrow, even if it is only an inch or two. This makes lining up of vital importance.

Often, if a fairway slopes from left to right, the green will do likewise, although this is not always the case. Therefore, try to view the green before you reach it. From the fairway it is much easier to see if the green slopes with the fairway or against it, or if it slopes from back to front or vice versa.

Once on the green, standing behind the ball is the best place to start the line up. From here a general view of the whole green and putt is attained. When standing behind the ball, look for the highest part of the green, and the lowest. Remember, the ball is round and will roll downhill.

If there is only one general borrow the putt is fairly straightforward to read. When the slope is from left to right, the putt needs to be hit left and the ball will roll down the slope from the left to right as it slows down. On a right to left slope the ball will do the opposite.

If there are many bumps in the green, then each section between the ball and the hole must be viewed separately.

On more difficult putts it is helpful to look from both the left and right sides, and from behind the hole.

The pace of the putt will depend on what sort of grass is on the green and how it has been cut, whether it is wet or dry and whether the putt is uphill or downhill.

The more information known about a green, the better your understanding of what will happen to the ball when you hit it. By taking time to look at all these points although you are not guaranteed to hole it, you will stand a better chance.

If you take care to look properly at the line of your putt, it does not mean that you take a long time. These things can easily be done so as to keep play moving quickly. The person furthest from the hole normally takes the longest time to line up the putt. The other golfers should be looking at their lines at the same time, and whilst one is putting, the others should be deciding what they are going to do when it is their turn. Unless you are interfering with the line of the person's putting, there is no need to wait until they have finished before you get ready to play.

VISUALIZE YOUR PUTTS

Once you have safely negotiated all the hazards on the way to the green, you will be faced with the problem of getting the ball into the hole in as few strokes as possible, and for many golfers that is the greatest hazard of all. There is nothing more annoying than hitting a difficult green, or hitting a great shot near the hole, and then missing the putt.

Putting is dominated by feel and visualization. The softer a putt is hit the more it will borrow; the harder a putt is hit, the less it will borrow. Learning to visualize what will happen when you hit the ball is important, because it is with that information that you will decide how hard and where to hit the putt. The longer and more difficult the putt, the more you will need to visualize what will happen to it.

If the ball has to go up and over a slope, or if there are several different dips and slopes between you and the hole, always try to imagine how the ball will react as it goes over each bump. Will the upslope slow the ball down? take it to the left? to the right? will the ball speed up as it goes down the other side? Try to visualize how fast the ball will roll and the effect each borrow is having on it. Then take your stance and have a practice putt, visualizing your

ball travelling towards the hole as you expect it to go. Let your eyes follow the line along the green which your ball is about to travel. Visualize the ball rolling along the green and going into the hole. Get a feel for how hard to hit the putt. Only when you have this firmly fixed in your head should you finally hit the putt.

KEEP IT LOW AND SLOW

Most good putters have very simple putting strokes which just take the putter head back from and through to the target along the ball-to-target line.

A squarely hit putt, which makes contact with the ball at the lowest part of the putting arc, will hit the ball so that it hugs the ground and has a greater chance of staying on line.

If the putter is picked up quickly in the back stroke, it is likely to be a steep stroke which will cause the ball to jump off the putter head and not run smoothly to the hole. Putting with this sort of action also makes it difficult to judge distance, as the putt is almost hit with backspin.

If the putting stroke is too short for the length of putt you will have to speed up the stroke to get the ball to the hole. This speeding up will cause a jerky movement and the ball will not come off the putter head consistently or smoothly.

If there is a lot of wrist movement in your putting stroke, or your hands come through and hit the ball before the arms, the putting stroke is less likely to be consistent. The ball will not run smoothly because the putt was not hit at the bottom of the arc.

By thinking Low and Slow, I make sure my putting stroke starts back low to the ground so that I don't make a choppy putting stroke which would make the ball jump off the putter head. By taking it back slowly, I can keep my hands and arms moving back together. If it is a short putt I take the putter back a short distance, and if it is a long putt I will take it back further, depending on how far I want the ball to go. Putting in this way keeps a smooth tempo and keeps the ball running smoothly towards the hole.

TIP 63 WATCH THE HOLE

'Keep your eye on the ball' is probably the most used of the sporting clichés. In golf it is important to look at the ball because our heads have to stay still as we swing. It is so easy to become fixated by watching the ball that we forget we have to hit it towards a target. Unless, whilst looking at the ball, you can sense the direction that the ball should travel and how hard to hit it, you will not hit a good putt.

The better player you become, the easier it will be to visualize what is going to happen to the ball after you have hit it. When a dart player throws the dart, he will focus on where he wants the dart to hit, a javelin thrower will focus on where the javelin will fly. From time to time I practise putting not looking at the ball, but focusing on the hole instead.

Try putting for a few minutes looking at the hole instead of the ball. Set up as you would normally, leaving yourself a ten-foot putt. Before you take the putter head back, look towards the hole, focusing your attention on it rather than the ball. Whilst still looking at the hole hit the ball towards it. Most golfers mis-hit the first few putts when they try this, but continue and you will soon hit them better and probably hole quite a few.

The benefit of this drill is that it will turn your attention away from the mechanics of the putting stroke and make you focus on the hole and how the ball is rolling. After all, that is where you want the ball to go. It will also help you to become slightly more relaxed over the ball, as your thoughts are focused on the hole and not your putting stroke or the ball itself.

TIP 64 — EYES OVER THE BALL

If you are going to try this drill it is important that you know which is your dominant eye.

Use this technique. With both eyes open point at something at least 20 feet away. Close first your left eye. Is your finger still on the target or has it moved to the side? Open **your left eye and then close your right eye. Is the finger on the target, or has it moved to the side? Whichever eye sees the finger staying nearest to the target is your dominant eye, and should be above the ball when you putt.**

One of the reasons for poorly hit putts is that your head is not squarely over the ball.

If your head is behind the ball at address, it is very likely your shoulders will be tilted or aiming a little to the right and your putting stroke will follow this line, the bottom of the arc of the putting stroke will be behind, instead of at the ball, and you will not get a good square strike.

If your head is in front of the ball at address, your shoulders will probably be tilted or aiming left, and the stroke will be across the line, the bottom of the arc of the putting stroke will be ahead of the ball, again causing a badly hit putt. How badly you strike the ball will depend on how much your body has moved in relation to the ball. If your head has only slightly moved, it will probably not affect your body position and therefore the putt will be all right. However, if it has severely moved it is almost impossible to hit the ball correctly.

The best position from which to putt is with your dominant eye directly over the ball, which will in turn centre your body and bring the strike at the lowest point in the arc of

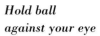

*Hold ball
against your eye*

*Let it
drop to the
ground*

*Putt from where
the ball first
landed*

the putting stroke, aiding a good sound putt.

Take your stance as if you were going to putt. Before you hit the putt hold a ball against your dominant eye, let it drop to the ground, and mark where it first touched the ground. If it is not in the middle of your stance, for instance if it drops to the right of your right foot, it shows that your body is severely out of line; you need to put a couple of clubs down and use them to get lined up correctly. Once you have aligned your body correctly, repeat the process of dropping a ball from your eye, and where the ball lands shows where your head is positioned and where your eyes will be when you putt. By continuing to practise with your dominant eye directly over the ball it should improve the strike and roll of your putts.

TIP 65 MAKE EVERY PUTT A SIX-INCH PUTT

If you can always hole putts from six inches then why can't you always hole them from a foot, or three feet or even ten feet? Part of the problem is confidence. You expect to hole every putt from six inches, but you don't expect to hole every putt from ten feet. Good putters look as though they can hole a putt from anywhere, and often look disap-

pointed at missing even the long difficult putts.

Another of the reasons for problems is not lining up correctly. When putting from very close to the hole you can see the hole and your putter, lining up is easy, you can't miss. But when you start to get further from the hole, and borrows begin to play a part in the direction the ball will roll, it gets more difficult to line up correctly.

In lining up shots from the fairway, if you just address the ball and look towards the target it will be difficult to line up correctly. However, by picking something just in front of the ball it is much easier to line up the clubhead and visualize the direction that the ball is about to take. This is the same in putting. If you pick something just in front of the ball to aim at, it is easier to putt. In essence, you make every putt a six-inch putt if you aim at something six inches in front of your ball.

All you have to do on a long putt is line the putt up, then choose something six inches in front of the ball on that line and concentrate on hitting the ball over that point with the right pace.

To give you confidence to putt this way, work through this drill on the putting green.

With six balls, find as straight a putt as possible. At about one foot from the hole, place two tees a hole's width apart. Take your stance six inches from the tees and concentrate on putting through the tees to the hole. Move back another foot each time you hole six in a row, all the time keeping the tees six inches in front of you.

In practising this drill you will build up your confidence, and when you are on the course if you aim at a spot six inches in front of the ball it will make putting much easier.

CHAPTER 9

Short Game

 **BACKSPIN**

During the ladies' clinics I give I try to involve those watching. I encourage everyone to ask questions. On one particular day, a lady watching asked: 'How can I stop the ball on the green when I am playing over a bunker with a 3 wood?' I asked what her handicap was, it was 36.

Having a realistic idea what you can and can't do depending on your handicap, strength and golfing ability is important if you are to get the most from your game. To this lady, I gave the simple answer: 'YOU CAN'T'. If you have a high handicap it is unrealistic to expect to hit a 9 iron or even a wedge and expect backspin.

A ball will stop on a green for a variety of reasons – the shot is played into the wind, the green is soft, a high shot has been hit so that it lands softly, and lastly backspin is applied to the ball by the hitting technique.

Backspin is achieved by a firm descending blow to the back of the ball which squeezes the ball forward. Most women don't hit the ball hard enough to get backspin. Even many women professionals don't hit the ball hard enough with anything other than the short irons to get a noticeable amount of backspin. Because most amateurs struggle for distance they do not need to get the ball to stop.

If it is important for me to hit a shot with backspin I really try to hit down hard and firmly whilst trying to maintain a solid left-hand position through impact as long as possible.

If you feel that it is important for you to get backspin, and your handicap and strength are adequate, start by hitting down with your wedge on the back of the ball, leading through the ball with your hands. Once you can fly the wedge in and get it to check, try the action with lower clubs.

TIP 67 CHIP LIKE YOU PUTT

Chipping is a vital part of the game because when other parts are going wrong it is good play around the green that can get you out of trouble and save your score.

What I enjoy about the short game is learning to manufacture different shots.

I know, however, that many golfers have such a fear of short shots around the green that chipping becomes a nightmare, and so worried are they by past experiences that they tense up too much and can't play a smooth shot. In order to play shots properly from around the green it is helpful to think of chipping as being an extension of the putting stroke.

The most important thing to remember is that the loft on the club will make the ball go up in the air, you never need to help the ball up. All that happens when most golfers try to get the ball up in the air is that they thin the shot and it races to the other side of the green.

Like the putting stroke, the chip should be played with a smooth pendulum swing, and the length of swing will depend on how far the ball has to go. Don't take it back a long way and have to slow down before impact as this will cause a duff shot.

The club should be held firmly but not too tightly or your arms will be tense, and if the club is held too loosely you will get a sloppy shot.

Once you have an idea of the technique, you need to practise to build up confidence.

A good way to do this is to line up ten balls on the edge of the green, hit them one after another, without stopping, to see where they finish, thinking only about your tempo. Then hit ten chips with your right hand only holding the club, and then repeat with your left hand. Next hit ten chips concentrating on how far you want the ball to go, making sure with these ten that you line up between each shot.

If you are not chipping well, don't put any pressure on yourself. See if you can do the above drill three times a week, either at the golf course or towards a bucket in the garden. Until you feel you are hitting them well don't worry about how the shots are going. Remember, we all improve at different speeds so take your time and just enjoy learning to control the club.

Trying too hard and expecting too much too soon will only result in despondency. So persevere at your own pace and you'll probably surprise yourself.

TIP 68 LEARN THE LOB

There are so many bunkers around most greens that it is inevitable your ball will finish behind one at some stage when you are playing. If the pin is not directly over the other side of the bunker you will not have to go over it. However, there are times when you will be faced with the decision of how to get on to the green without going into the bunker.

The beginner or high handicap golfer would be excused if she played around the bunker rather than risking going into it. However, if you are going to get your handicap down, you will eventually need to learn to lob the ball up.

The problem most golfers have when they try to get the ball to go up in the air is that instead of allowing the loft on the club to lift the ball, they actually lift their bodies up, producing a thinned shot that either goes straight into the bunker face or whizzes over the other side of the green. Other golfers are so aware that they need to hit down on the ball that they either hit down hard behind and so duff the ball a few feet, or hit much too hard.

To try and get the feeling of how your body, and in particular your hands, works when lobbing a ball over the bunker, try taking a ball in your right hand, stand with the bunker between you and the hole, and throw the ball over the bunker. Then take your stance as you would

to play a shot and try throwing another ball over.

You will notice that as you release the ball your body faces the hole naturally, and your shoulders come found and face the target without tilting. There is no sudden jerk. You take your arm back away from the target, and then swing it towards the target, releasing the ball as you come through.

Next take your sand wedge, and with a slightly open stance and club-face try keeping your weight towards the left side and hold your body quite still. Tighten the last two fingers in your left hand and the index finger and thumb in your right hand; this will help you to focus on what your hands are doing. Try the

same sort of swing as you did without a club, paying special attention not to help the ball up. Rely on your swing, co-ordination and the loft of the club.

If you start having problems playing the lob it is very easy to lose confidence and become tense. When this happens revert to throwing a few balls and build up the swing action from the start again.

TIP 69 USE YOUR BIG MUSCLES FROM THE BUNKER

Most lady golfers have a fear of bunkers. If you do not, you are fortunate, and in the minority. Men seem to assume that women will have a better short game, their reasoning being that women have more feel. However, although women might have a lot of feel, to play firmly hit chip shots you also need to be strong!

Examples of this principle are illustrated by the numerous 'Gentle Giants', such as Severiano Ballesteros, a prodigious hitter of the golf ball and a maestro around the green. In women's golf Laura Davies has enormous strength, and is arguably one of the longest hitters of a golf ball in women's golf, yet the subtleness she displays when faced with delicate lobs is inspiring.

Worries about bunkers often come from past experience of bad play. There are two common misconceptions with short shots, and in particular bunker shots. There is a tendency to help the ball up and an inclination to break the wrists early, which causes a flick at the ball. If your method is like this your bunker play will not be consistent, and the club will probably either come right under the ball and leave it in the bunker, or hit the middle of the ball and thin the shot.

It is true that there might be times when a quicker wrist break is called for, but generally ladies need a technique that will get the ball out every time, and as most are not too strong in their hands and arms, it is

the strong muscles of the upper body, the shoulders, which should play a bigger part.

Take your stance in the bunker, with your feet and shoulders aiming slightly to the left of the target. Place the ball and your hands forward in your stance, but make sure you don't tilt your shoulders to do this. Keeping your wrists very firm, begin to swing back, initiating the turn with your arms and shoulders. Concentrate on keeping a smooth and even tempo, don't break your wrists, swing down and through the sand to the top of the follow through using your **strong** muscles to propel the club through the sand. You can experiment with how far forward the ball can be placed, and the length of your back swing.

By learning to use your strong muscles, you can develop a firm hit and still play with feel.

 **TIP 70**

SEVEN IRON OVER THE TIER

When you are faced with a shot from the edge of the green where your ball has to negotiate a steep slope or tier, there are a variety of shots that you could use.

You can choose to hit your sand wedge and pitch it all the way up to the pin. Alternatively you could hit your wedge into the tier and make it jump up. You can also land the ball at the base of the tier and let it bounce up. However, the aforementioned are among those which carry a high penalty for any misjudgement. For instance, if you hit your sand wedge and aim to hit the ball onto the top tier but slightly underhit the shot it will not roll up the tier but will roll back down the slope away from the hole. I try to keep things as simple as possible, and play the shot that stands the best percentage chance of coming off. If I don't need to carry all the way up to the pin, I don't. I try to evaluate what is the worst that could happen to the ball and what would be the best.

Time after time I resort to using a 7 or 8 iron to hit a ball over a large tier in the green. I have even on occasion used these clubs on the green. But before you all go off and take divots from the greens and have the wrath of greenkeeper and committee come upon you, I would stress that those occasions when I would hit an iron from the green are very rare, and the slope on the green was too extreme to allow any feel with my putter.

The reason I say 7 and not putter is because the 7 iron will not have to be hit as hard as you would have to hit a putt, and it is therefore easier to get feel when playing the shot. I don't try to pitch the ball very far onto the green, I try to get it rolling

as quickly as possible. I usually pick a spot just in front of the ball and hit the ball for that spot. Before I hit the 7 iron I will visualize the direction the ball will go, whether the slope will change the direction in which the ball is travelling, or whether it will continue straight. The swing I put on the shot will be a short crisp action keeping my hands ahead of the clubface. Because the ball is rolling without backspin it will easily run up the tier to the pin.

HIT FROM THE TOE

Traditionally British golf courses have influenced the design of golf courses all over the world. Nowadays the reverse seems to be happening. New courses being built have little in common with the great British links such as St Andrews, Troon, Saunton or the inland courses of Woodall Spa, Sunningdale and The Berkshire. Since the introduction of fairway sprinklers, even the characteristics of these courses have changed.

When we watch the British Open, it is not the brown, weather-beaten, sunburnt links, but the green well-watered American-style links. With these changes, have come other foreign traits, one example of this being rough grown to the edge of the green requiring a lofted shot over the band of rough to reach the green. Not every new course has this problem, but if you play abroad or at many different courses in this country, it is something you will come up against.

When playing a more traditional course, the shots and clubs you may use to play chip shots from around the green are numerous. If hitting from six-inch-high thick rough, your options are few.

To get the ball up out of thick rough quickly enough to make it stop on the green there is really only one club that allows you to achieve this, and that is the sand wedge. However, even the sand wedge can get stuck in heavy rough, causing the clubface to close at impact and the ball either to come out very fast and low, or, even worse, not to come out at all.

When in this situation, try raising your hands to a more upright position at address and then aim to hit the ball out of the toe of the club. Try keeping your wrists very firm and make sure you hit through the shot crisply.

By doing this you will get less bounce from the clubface and the ball will not come out so speedily or run so far on landing.

TIP 72 — THE LAZY LOB

All through this book, and in nearly every book you may read or lesson you will have, the importance of accelerating the clubface into the ball is stressed.

There is one exception to this rule, not to be tried by beginners, and that is what I call the lazy lob.

Either through a bad shot, unlucky bounce or wrong clubbing you can find yourself with a shot up on to a raised green where there is little room to land and stop the ball. What you want is a shot that will get height but with little or no roll.

Depending on the situation, how I am playing, how the ball is lying and how confident I am, I may choose to play a lazy lob. By this I mean that the shot will feel as though I am swinging lazily. I take an open stance with an open clubface then make a long, slow swing, cutting across the ball slightly, and do not accelerate coming into the ball. I almost try to slow my swing down. This has the effect of making the ball land without any spin as if you were holding the ball out at arm's length and just letting the ball fall to the ground, dead. There is no 'HIT' at impact, although I still follow through towards the target to complete the swing.

I will only play this shot if I have

been practising it, and it is risky because it means flopping at the ball, almost in the way you duff a shot. Nevertheless, I have found that on countless occasions, when those watching thought I had no chance of getting the ball close to the pin, I was able to play this shot.

I must stress again: this is a shot that only those with good club control should attempt, and then only after practice.

THE TEXAS WEDGE

The 'TEXAS WEDGE' refers to a shot played with the putter from a place where a wedge would normally be used.

Many golfers resort to using their putters from a long way short of the green because they are worried about their chipping, and think they might duff or thin the shot if they play it with the wedge. However, this shot need not be restricted to those with wedge problems.

There are many times when this is the most sensible shot to play.

For example, when the pin is cut close to the front edge of the green, or on tight links fairways when you have a bad lie and when there is a closely mown hump between you and the pin.

The shot should be played very similarly to any other putt, but you will need to have a longer swing and hit the ball harder.

The most important thing when playing this shot is that you get a good square hit on the back of the ball. If you mis-hit the ball it will not travel far enough to get close to the pin.

Address the ball with your stance a little open, make sure your arms are relaxed and can swing back and through freely; allow a little flexing of your wrists, as you would in a longer swing. Play the shot with a pendulum action, making very sure to keep your body still and your head over the ball. Visualize how the ball will roll before you hit the shot, and once you are over the ball just concentrate on the distance. Although getting the right line is important, more important is the length. If you are a little off line but get the length right you will not be too far away; but if you get the line right and the length wrong it rarely results in an easy second putt.

ON THE BANK: HITTING DOWN

If your ball finishes above the hole on a bank that slopes down to the green it is important to play a shot that has maximum control. The face of the club will not be on the ball for long, because the slope is away from you. From this position it is very easy to hit a thin or hit into the ground behind the ball. It is more important with this shot to have a crisply hit shot and not be frightened to hit the ball quite hard with a very short swing.

It is important first of all to get your balance right, keep your weight firmly on your left leg, and it must stay rock solid. Try to adjust your shoulders so that they stay on a similar line to the slope. Put the ball back in your stance and your hands forward. From this position take the club back a short distance and try hitting the ball down the slope. If you try and lift it you will thin it, but by continuing down, you will give the loft on the club maximum chance to bring the ball up.

Don't attempt to hit the shot until you have a secure balance

TIP 75 ON THE BANK: HITTING UP

Often banks surrounding greens are closely mown, and a ball will not finish half-way up or down. However, occasionally the grass is longer and therefore requires a shot that will get the ball up quickly, over the bank, out of the rough and on to the green.

With a steep slope in front of the ball, it is impossible to have a normal follow through and so I play an explosion shot and *use* the upslope. I play the shot with my hands and arms, and try to hit the club straight into the bank just behind the ball, which makes the ball pop straight up.

Take your stance with the left knee well bent to allow for the bank. Settle yourself on the bank so that you do not lose your balance. It is extremely important to get a precise hit, so don't attempt the shot until your balance is secure. Play the ball towards the right foot, and hold club down the grip to give more control. Take the club back without any body movement, just hands and arms, and swing down into the ball hitting at the back of it firmly. Remember, the upslope in front of the ball will stop any follow through unless you try scooping the ball.

If you experiment with how far to take the club back and how hard you can hit into the bank you will soon learn to judge the distance.

TIP 76 — PLUGGED IN THE BUNKER

Most golfers assume that from a plugged lie in the bunker an open clubface will get the ball out. In fact it is quite the opposite. If you attempt to play the shot with an open clubface it will drag in the sand and you will not hit through and make a big enough explosion to get the ball out.

So, the first thing to remember when you are in a plugged lie is to close the clubface and put your hands forward.

The second most important thing to remember when hitting this shot is that you make the club swing at a steep angle. If the clubhead enters the sand in a shallow or flat angle you are likely to catch only the top of the ball and it will probably be thinned. The feeling you want is a pick up and chop down into the sand, producing power into the shot which is necessary to get the ball out. Put the ball towards the back of your stance and lean very slightly forward.

The only problem with this shot is that it comes out of the sand with no backspin, and so will run a long way, making it difficult to judge how hard to hit it and how far it will run.

Hopefully, you will not find yourself plugged too often, but when you are, don't be greedy. Getting out first time is the primary concern, then you worry about the next shot.

PART FOUR

CHAPTER 10

Trouble Shooting

LEARN TO PRACTISE FOR TROUBLE

Are you ever envious when you watch professionals playing on television, and they hit incredible shots from what might seem an impossible lie in the trees or bushes? Do you wonder how they can do it? Remember Bernhard Langer climbing a tree and playing a shot whilst perched in the branches? And Severiano Ballesteros winning the British Open from the car park and various other places not normally visited by golfers? If you do, then there are two things to remember: Firstly, most professional golfers are extremely strong in their hands and arms; and secondly, they will only attempt something if they have tried it in practice. It might seem to you that they are manufacturing a new shot never tried before, but believe me, they will have tried in practice nearly every shot they and you could possibly imagine.

I learnt this very early in my golf career. When I was an amateur I used to spend time in Portugal practising during the winter. Several players from the men's tour would also practise there, and during one winter, every afternoon, for about six weeks Brian Evans, Gordon Brand, Pip Barry and I would have a chipping competition. The loser would buy tea. We would each take it in turns to choose where we would hit from, the nearest to the pin winning the point, and the first to five or ten would win the match. The places we would chip from would start off fairly straightforward, from the edge of the green or over a bunker. Then as we began to increase feel, our imaginations would be let loose and we would put the balls in bushes, behind trees, on greenkeeper's cuttings, on paths, in divots, anywhere we could think of. I even remember a spiky plant with needle-like points - if you pushed a balata ball on to the point it would stay there; it looked like a ball tree. By attempting these shots we were achieving more than a fun practice session, we were also learning feel, co-ordination and a flare for playing shots out of what might have seemed an impossible position.

You don't need to go to Portugal to practise in this way, you can have a chipping competition on any green, practice field or garden. If you aren't using a chipping green aim at a bucket or umbrella. It's more enjoyable if you have someone to play against, and although you might be horrendous at first from what might seem silly places, you will get a better feel for what you can and can't do. The next time you find yourself somewhere you shouldn't be, it may be you can save par and have others around you wondering how you did it.

TIP 78 — OUT OF THE ROUGH

No golfer aims to hit a ball into the rough purposely. However, if you play golf it is a certainty that from time to time you will find yourself in the rough.

Lady golfers generally find it more difficult to hit from the rough than do men. The stronger you are

in your hands and arms, the easier and further you can hit from the rough. But remember, a well hit 8 iron can go further than a badly struck 4 iron.

The first priority when you are hitting from the rough is to get the ball out. Don't bite off more than you can chew. If it is thick rough you might have to aim sideways to get it back to the fairway, but it's better to use up one shot and get the ball in play and in a position that you can hit to the green than to attempt something silly and waste shots – remember every shot counts.

The safest club to hit out of the rough is the sand wedge. The loft on the sand wedge will ensure as good a contact as possible with the ball and lift it quickly. The weight of the sand wedge will help you get to the bottom of the rough.

Play the ball back in your stance and make sure you hit well through the shot. Do not stop when you reach the ball, try following through. Push your hands slightly further forward as this will promote the more upright swing needed to chop through the rough. As with any shot, keep your eye on the ball and your body still.

If you have a practice swing away from the ball you will see how easy or difficult the shot you are attempting will be. If you do feel your shots from the rough are not going well, try the next tip.

TIP 79 — SWING IN THE ROUGH

Former Long Ashton professional Wally Smithers was well known for saying 'It's all in the 'ands'. He professed that if your hands were strong enough, you could do almost anything with the golf ball. Those who knew him wouldn't dispute the fact, as he was renowned for being able to hit a shot over his head and land the ball behind him.

To get strong hands he would tell everyone, especially all the juniors, to go into the rough with a club and just swing backwards and forwards.

This is an excellent form of practice as it not only strengthens your hands and arms, but will give you an idea of how hard you will have to hit the ball to get it out of the rough. This can be tried in the rough on the practice ground or along the hedges on the golf course.

It is also a good idea to hit a few shots out of thick rough after you have tried the drill. However, I would advise you to stay off the course if you are attempting to hit shots.

TIP 80 — AWKWARD STANCE

There are very few courses where you are lucky enough to play every shot on flat ground. Learning to play shots when the ball is beneath your feet, on an uphill lie, a down hill lie, etc., is vital if you are hoping to improve.

There are basic fundamentals which must be understood when hitting shots from various slopes.

Ball below your feet

When the ball is below your feet try keeping your weight towards your heels, and keep your legs a little more rigid than you would normally do. You should aim a little left, as the shot will normally move from left to right. If you take up your regular stance it will be difficult to hit the ball correctly, therefore bend forward and flex your knees a little more than you would usually. Due to the fact that you are standing awkwardly, it is not likely that you will strike the shot as well as you would from a flat lie, especially if it is on a severe slope.

Ball above your feet

Make sure your weight is forward so that you don't fall back down the slope. Aim a little right, as the ball will usually draw. If you swing normally, you are likely to hit the slope and not the ball so try swinging slightly more round yourself in a flatter than usual plane. Lastly, when the ball is on an upslope it is slightly nearer to you, so grip down the shaft a little.

Although these are the basic fundamentals, I have a 1, 2, 3 check list for these type of shots.

1 When the ball is below your feet you will not be able to do the 'text book' swing. Concentrate on taking a steeper swing and focus on hands and arms. Don't think about hip and shoulder turn, especially on a severe slope.
2 When the ball is above your feet imagine you are swinging a baseball bat, and try taking a big shoulder turn. Don't then change your plane coming into the ball. Continue round in the follow through.
3 With both shots it is important to keep a still head and not try to hit the ball too hard.

TIP 81

PLAYING BACKWARDS

If you are unfortunate enough to finish up against a tree where you can't hit the ball with your regular swing you might consider playing the shot left-handed. It will need a little practice and shouldn't be tried on the golf course until perfected, or at least until you feel confident of hitting the ball each time.

When I play a left-handed shot I put my left hand below my right. The left hand is now the one I would rely on for direction and strength. I find it easier for the left hand to be dominant as the palm of the left hand is facing the target. Next I will turn the club around so that it lies with the toe to the ground and the face pointing in the direction that you want the ball to go. I pay special attention to making sure I watch the ball during my swing.

I would use any club from a sand wedge to 6 iron, depending on the lie and how far I want the ball to go. If you play the shot with a sand wedge you can still get loft on the shot, and if you practise you can hit the ball quite a long way, which in some cases will get you out of trouble.

AWKWARD LIES

There are basic fundamentals which must be understood when hitting shots up or down slopes.

Downhill lie

Try to get your shoulders parallel to the slope enabling you to swing as normally as possible. Position the ball towards the higher foot. Don't allow your body to sway down the slope when you swing, keep your head very still and your left leg very firm whilst still allowing a turn. When deciding which club you will hit, remember that the loft on the face will be decreased, i.e. an 8 iron will have the loft of a 7 or 6 iron, the 6 iron will have the loft of the 5 or 4, and so on.

Uphill lie

In the same way as you set your shoulders parallel to the downhill slope, when hitting from an uphill lie your shoulders should also be parallel and the ball should be positioned towards the higher foot. Your body should not fall back when you swing, so make sure your head is still, and (for the right-handed golfer) your right leg firm. The loft on your club has increased, the 8 iron will have the loft of the 9 and so on.

It has been my experience that a few things need to be added, especially for the female golfer, and my 1, 2, 3 check list is:

1 Although on a down slope your club face has lost loft, it will not necessarily mean you hit the ball further. Men are very strong in their hands and arms and might hit the ball further, women just tend to hit it lower, so if you have to carry the ball a long way, don't think of changing clubs.
2 On a down slope try to continue your follow through down the slope a little longer than you would normally. Don't try to get the ball up in the air, as you are only likely to thin it.
3 On an up slope let the clubhead follow the slope up, don't swing into the slope unless, of course, one leg is up on a bank and the other is on flat ground. Then you will only be able to hit into the bank with a lofted club and the ball will pop up in the air.

There is a problem in practising these shots, as although there are steep slopes on the course, most practice grounds and all driving ranges are flat, and so trying to work on improving technique is difficult.

The only way round this is to go on the golf course when it's quiet, with a couple of balls. Try the awkward lies and experiment and see how it is best for you to hit the ball.

DOWNHILL LIE
Far left: Shoulders parallel to the slope

Left: Keep head still

UPHILL LIE
Far left: Don't try to get the ball up in the air

Left: Maintain balance through the ball

Far right: Keep head still

Shoulders parallel to slope

Secure stance –

Increased loft –

Far right: Don't fall backwards down hill. Keep secure stance

CHAPTER 11

Getting the Most from your Game

 **KEEP IT SIMPLE OFF THE TEE**

The teeing area, and in particular the first tee, plays an important part in setting the theme for how you feel during the round of golf.

If you hit a good shot, straight down the middle, you will feel good. If, though, you hit out of bounds, into a bunker or the trees or you mis-hit your first shot of the day, you will not be in such a positive frame of mind.

Many ladies get embarrassed by their tee shots, wanting to get them over with as quickly as possible. For this reason they seldom take their time, and bad shots often occur which affect their confidence and can affect them for the rest of the round.

Most golfers, whether top class professionals or beginners, take a few holes to feel they are relaxed and playing well. It is one thing warming up on the range, and another actually playing the game. It takes a few shots to get into your game, to get your mind switched on to scoring. If you start with a series of bad shots, it is very easy to become discouraged and lose confidence, which can result in a bad day's play. I know players who after a bad first hole will say, "That's it, I'm not going to do very well today". If you convince yourself of that, then you will not do well.

If the most important thing when teeing off is to keep the ball in play you need not necessarily hit your driver. The driver is a difficult club to hit, and if you are not certain of hitting it well then leave it in the bag. Keep things as simple as possible. If you like your 5 wood or 7 iron, hit either of them from the tee. The important thing, especially for the higher handicap, is that you feel comfortable, relaxed and as confident as possible. Don't attempt to do anything that you are not sure you can do. Remember, it's better to hit a wedge off the tee and stay short of a difficult bunker than risk going into it and it ruining your score card.

The lower your handicap, the more important it will be to hit a long tee shot, and for the low handicap group it is their mental attitude as much as anything which will affect how the ball is struck.

Take plenty of practice swings before it is your turn to hit.

Think about swinging rhythmically, not rushing any part of your routine.

Choose a nice piece of grass on which to tee your ball. Take plenty of time lining your body up with wherever you choose to aim.

Picture in your mind hitting the ball and it flying down the middle.

Focus on where you want the ball to finish, not the place you don't want it to finish! It's no good repeating to yourself, "Don't go in the trees, don't go in the trees", because that is probably the first place the ball will go.

It is important that you don't flood your mind with thoughts of who might be watching you, whether it's the England selectors, the lady Captain or your husband. What they might be thinking about you or your swing is not what is important, it is the tee shot and where it is going that must take priority. Don't think about where you finished last time you played.

By choosing an easy club to hit

and keeping your mind focused on the positive you will immediately be more positive. The first tee can become a place you will enjoy, instead of, as it is for many lady golfers, the place they wish to leave as quickly as possible.

TIP 84   FOOT BALL

There is no doubt that generally women are not as strong as men, and in golf this means that they must have better swings because they do not have strength to compensate for a poorly executed shot. A man's physique, strong hands and arms, can still hit the ball a long way with a mis-hit shot. Most women are unable to do this.

It is therefore vitally important for the woman golfer to understand that to make a powerful hit at the ball, she must learn the correct foot, leg and body movement, and coordinate this with a sound tempo.

Although women are not as strong as men, they are a lot more supple, which can cause problems in learning the correct backswing.

Most women tilt or sway in their backswing, when what is needed is a pivot, coil or turn away from the ball. In trying to get their hips out of the way, many women actually slide laterally, making it impossible to implement the power that a proper turn builds up. This results in a choppy shot which lacks power and doesn't go as far as their strength should allow.

To help promote the turn as opposed to the sway you might like to try the following drill.

Put a ball under the outside of your right heel. This will immediately bring the weight to the inside of your right foot and leg. When you swing back think of your right hip moving back and turning. Your weight will remain on the inside of the right foot making it difficult for you to sway to the right or for your hips to move laterally. At the top of your backswing you will now have some resistance in your right leg. This will give you a feeling of being able to push off with the right leg when starting the down swing sequence of feet, legs, hips, shoulders, arms and hands, turning through the ball with the power of the whole body behind the shot.

TIP 85 — USE A NET

The winter months are an ideal time to work on your golf swing. It is, however, not always convenient to go to the golf course every day. Although in some ways winter might be the most logical, as you are probably playing less, it's also the worst time to summon up enthusiasm to go out on a muddy, windswept field and battle the elements for half an hour.

There are two ways round this. One is to go to a driving range and the other is to use a practice net.

A practice net is the ideal place to work on your golf swing or keep it swinging sweetly through the winter. The real advantage with a net as opposed to any other practice is that although you are hitting balls, the net stops the ball travelling any distance, and you therefore concentrate more on your swing and how it feels than where the ball has gone. This is of great importance when you are changing things in your swing. So often golfers only worry about what is happening to the ball, and will not change their swing if it means hitting the ball less well for a while. In a net, you focus on the swing faults you are trying to put right, and give little concern to what is happening to the ball.

Of course, how often you use the

net will depend on how motivated you are. It is advisable to put the net in a sheltered part of the garden, where you get a little protection. The ideal situation for a net is in a garage or an outbuilding with a high roof.

Some clubs have nets for golfers to use before they play, and this has to be a good idea. I would love to see more clubs having an indoor area where members can keep hitting inside when play is restricted outside.

TIP 86 — AT HOME ON THE RANGE

Using a driving range seems to be growing in popularity, and it is nice to see the numbers of ranges growing to cope with the increased demand.

Unfortunately, the benefits that golfers might gain from their use are badly restricted because of a lack of understanding of how to use them.

I must admit to being mildly amused when I see the droves, armed with drivers, commence their bag of balls and with great gusto, rapidly firing them off in quick succession, not stopping to take aim or check stance, etc.

What they don't seem to realize is that the benefits from ball bashing are minimal. It will only help you get

slightly stronger and improve your co-ordination.

Driving ranges are teaching establishments. You go to have a lesson, and practise what you have been taught. You go to hone your technique and work on strength and co-ordination.

The most common thing I hear from golfers who use ranges is that they hit the ball really well at the range but terribly once on the golf course.

To me, the reason for this is obvious. Most driving ranges are anywhere from 100 yards and upwards wide, there are probably a few flags dotted around, and several thousand golf balls awaiting collection. In contrast, the average fairway is fifty yards wide, the average green twenty yards wide. If you miss the green you know it. There is no thinking that you have hit a good shot simply because it was well hit, went up in the air and has gone a long way.

However, on the driving range you excuse the wild shot, and dwell more on how well it was struck and how far it has gone.

Notice next time you go to the range how many golfers, especially men, hit drivers as hard as they can. Then notice how straight they are going. Bragging how far you hit the ball will not help you when you want to play golf!

So, how can we use the driving range to maximum advantage?

1 If you have a bag of balls divide them up into four equal amounts, i.e. if there are eighty balls in the basket or bag divide them into groups of twenty.

   Hit the first twenty, with any short iron, just thinking about warming up.

2 Hit the next twenty working on your swing. If you are having lessons, work on whatever your professional was telling you. Make sure that you have clubs on the ground so that you are aiming correctly. If you are not having lessons, do a mental check of aim, grip, stance, posture, take away, etc . . .

3 Hit the next twenty with a sand wedge or pitching wedge, aiming at a target fifty yards away. See how many times you can hit the target, keep a mental note, and then try to beat that number next time. By aiming at a target you are increasing feel, co-ordination and putting pressure on yourself, in the same way that you would on the golf course when chipping to a green fifty yards away. The element of competition is brought in so that you will keep a record of how you improve, and will help to maintain your concentration and interest.

4 Hit the last twenty in groups of fives, aiming at different targets, and hitting different clubs. Line up as you would when playing on the course and give yourself a mark out of ten for how close to the green or pin (depending on your standard) you finish, i.e. ten points for hitting the target, no points for being twenty yards wide.

If you visit the range regularly, mix up your practice session further by working on the strengthening drills, etc.

By giving yourself a purpose whilst at the range, it will make your practice more interesting, you will have a record of how much you improve, and it will benefit your golf when you actually go out to play.

TIP 87 — USE THE LONGER CLUB WHEN UNDECIDED

In a dream round of golf you would only be faced with full shots of the exact distance for each club. You would never be faced with indecision.

Unfortunately, in reality this doesn't happen and the distance you have to hit is often between clubs. When faced with this decision, there are two choices. Either you try to hit the shorter of the two clubs and hit it harder than you would normally, or you hit the longer, and hit it lighter.

When faced with this decision, I usually take the longer club. My thinking behind this is that it's easier to maintain rhythm swinging smoothly and firmly, but the harder I hit the ball the more likely I am to mis-hit or lose accuracy.

There are two exceptions to my rule. One is from about 100 yards, when I would prefer to hit a hard wedge or 9 iron than hit more club. The other occasion when I would take the shorter club is if it is strongly down wind. Here again it is difficult to control an easy shot, as the wind might take it too far.

 ### TIP 88 PUNCH SHOTS

Control, consistency and good judgement are all prerequisite to playing the game of golf.

One of the most consistent and easily controllable shots I have ever learnt is the Punch Shot.

No golfer has a full armoury of shots until this one has been mastered. It is a must from tight lies, out of divots, playing in the wind and whenever it is important to have control.

The ball should be played further back in the stance, your hands a little further forward than they would normally be. Adopt a slightly open stance. When you take your stance hold your wrists very firm, swing back from the ball, taking only a three-quarter swing. From the top of the swing, get the feeling that you are punching down on the back of the ball and through to the target. You will still move your body out of the way by turning your hips, but you will have a restricted follow through. Maintain your hands in front of their normal position, and keep them moving towards the target. Tempo is as important in this shot as any other, and you should take one club more than you normally would so that you can keep an even tempo and hit a smooth punch shot not a rushed one.

Hitting the ball with this technique will make it travel lower than it normally would, which makes it an ideal shot to use when you don't want the ball to go high, i.e. when hitting under a tree or in windy conditions where a high hit shot will be affected and often move off line much. By keeping your hands forward in the swing the shot normally stays very straight.

Hitting the ball with a punch shot is the best way to get out of a divot. If you attempt a normal shot to get out of a divot, it is almost impossible to get any control on the ball, but by hitting firmly down on the ball you will gain maximum control.

THOUGHTFUL PLAY TO THE GREEN

Whatever your standard you will usually be able to find various options to play to the green, some sensible and some not so sensible one. How you proceed will depend on how confident you are, your standard of golf and the way the hole is constructed and its hazards.

As an example: if you have a bunker between your ball and the pin, you have three possible options.

1 You hit away from it.
2 You hit into it.
3 You hit over it on to the green.

Your response to this situation would depend on the following:

The high handicap player

If it is a deep bunker most high handicap golfers will have trouble getting the ball out; so it should be avoided at all costs.

By considering going in to the bunker, you are not being negative, you are being realistic. If the bunker is small the first option is to play around. However, if the bunker runs all around the front and side, you are eventually going to have to go over it. Deciding when, either from close up or further away, will depend on how good your wedge shots are and how close you think you can get to the bunker without going into it. You must begin to think this way, not just say to yourself, 'It's a 7 iron shot. I'll aim for the pin and hit the 7.' Golf is a game of tactics, and knowing your strengths and weaknesses can save you shots.

Lower handicap players

These players should not be so bothered by bunkers in front of greens, unless the pin is directly over the other side and cut near to the bunker. It then becomes a matter of judgement. Should you go for the pin and risk the occasional shot going in the bunker, or should you play for the middle of the green? If you are a super bunker player it is probably an easy decision. However, most golfers are not, and must be constantly reminded that even when they have taken the chance and played the shot correctly they are not guaranteed to hole the putt. There are times when it is better to leave a 15–20 foot putt, where you don't have to play from the bunker and at least stand the chance of putting, than risk hitting into trouble and ruining your score card.

Each player must decide when to go for the pin, and when to go for the middle of the green.

Don't be fixated by the pin. Consider the alternatives.

Becoming a better player will depend on thoughtful approach shots as much as good swing technique.

FORGET THE BAD

TIP 90

Golf is not a game where you perfect a swing, go out and play and everything goes well. Unfortunately, what often happens is that you are swinging well, go out to play – and come in with a bad score.

Learning to be thoughtful, considering all the options, being disciplined and making the most of every opportunity are what separates the top players from the rest.

On the practice ground most professionals look good. They hit the ball well and seem to know what they are doing. How is it then that some score well, and some fade away?

If it were just a case of having a good swing, the order of merit tables would be very different. I always say **being a professional isn't about playing well or swinging well. No, it is about grinding a score out when you are not playing well**. Anyone can score well when everything is going well, but it takes a player of character and determination to succeed when all seems against them.

I love it when I've played badly and someone says, 'Oh, good score. You must have hit it well today.' I say, 'No, I hit the ball badly, but I scored well.'

Every player reacts differently when they hit bad shots. Some get aggressive and use bad language and hurl clubs, others seem not to care at all. Most beginners get terribly frustrated. I know I did, I would get so disappointed after practising hard all week only to play terribly in the medal. It doesn't seem fair and it probably isn't.

If I have learnt anything since starting to play golf, then it is how to react when in a frustrating, disappointing, disheartening situation on the golf course. My thought process is this. Did I mean to hit the ball where I have done? Did I try my hardest on the shot? Did I concentrate? Am I infallible?

There is an old saying 'BETTER TO HAVE FOUGHT AND LOST THAN NEVER FOUGHT AT ALL.'

If I have tried and failed, there is no disgrace if a shot's gone wrong and it's cost me, my only concern is, did I give it my best? If the answer is YES, I forget it. It has happened and the important thing is to focus quickly on the next shot.

However, if the reason I hit a bad shot was through not taking time to line up, check my yardage, note wind direction, etc., then I would get a little annoyed with myself, making sure, at least for the rest of the round, that I didn't hurry again.

We need to accept that we will all have bad days. However, if I've done the best 76 I could have done on a bad day then I will take satisfaction in that. Others around me will not dictate how I should feel after a round of golf. They might say the score is terrible, but I will know it could have easily been an 80.

Next time you are playing in a competition, and have prepared properly but things are not going well, forget the bad shots, try your hardest, give it your best and take pleasure in what you have been able to achieve that day, even if it's not what other people were expecting of you.

COPY THE PROS

When I first started playing golf I used to enjoy watching the Colgate Ladies Tournament played at Sunningdale. I distinctly remember one Saturday as if it were yesterday. I had been watching Nancy Lopez, who was leading the tournament. I thought she had tremendous tempo. When the golf had finished I went up to the golf club to play a few holes. My handicap was about 18. In my mind I could see how she would

swing the club, I could visualize her rhythm and timing, the way she stood to the ball, her concentration and professionalism, and I tried to imitate it. I don't think for one minute that my swing suddenly looked like hers, or that I was transformed into a professional looking player. However, whatever I was doing, it was the best I had ever hit the ball, and the best I had ever scored round those few holes.

I have found that throughout my career, watching good players with good swings, tempo, rhythm, has been beneficial. I don't have to swing like they do, or hit the ball as hard, but I know that I have learnt a lot.

If you get the chance to go to a professional tournament, try spending an hour before you go home watching the professionals on the practice ground. Watch their tempo; how they stand to the ball. Watch what they are working on. If you are not able to get to a tournament, watch television. Notice how the top players never rush anything, they take their time, choosing the right club, having a practice swing, taking their stance and playing the shot.

Whatever your standard, if you get the chance, try playing with golfers who are better than you. If you get the chance to play with a professional, even better; stand close and see how they address the

large number of the more competitive women golfers.

There is no doubt, hitting the ball a long way has its advantages. You hit less club into the green, you can reach the par fives in two and you can often intimidate your opponent.

However, with these advantages come a few disadvantages. The further you hit the ball, the narrower the fairway becomes, the more accurate your line has to be and the more likely you are to get into trouble.

You don't have to know a lot about the game to see how most golfers try to get the ball to go further. You can watch them on the tee, muscles bursting as they launch their bodies into what is usually a badly timed mis-hit shot. By simply turning up the muscular force you will not hit the ball further. The key elements in driving distance are firstly a reliable technique, timing, co-ordination, and lastly correctly applied strength. Most amateurs fail to hit a long shot when they need to because they are concentrating on the wrong thing. When they are not so bothered about hitting the ball a long way they relax, swing the club more accurately and hit the ball further.

ball, where they aim the ball on the clubface, where their weight is distributed at address and how they line up their shots. Have a look through their golf bag to see what sort of clubs they use.

Then go away and play, trying to picture what you have seen in your mind. By visualizing their swings, and trying to copy what you have seen, it will not transform your swing but it can immediately transform your game.

TIP 92 GETTING DISTANCE WITH YOUR DRIVES

The average male golfer seems preoccupied with hitting the ball further, and so do most juniors and a

Hitting the ball a long way with your driver starts as you address the ball. When you take your stance it is important that you are well balanced and relaxed.

In order to accumulate power in the backswing your clubhead, hands, shoulders and hips should move away from the ball at the same time. Do not allow any part of your body to rush off on its own. In fact many top golfers actually try to swing more slowly when they want the ball to go further. By doing this they ensure that a really good full shoulder turn is achieved. Your shoulders should turn ninety degrees and the width created between your hands and shoulders at address should be maintained. Your wrists should cock ninety degrees during the backswing.

The downswing should be equally as smooth as the backswing; no part of the body should move 'out of turn'. If your shoulders turn through before the rest of the body, you will come across the ball and hit it off line with less power because you have not hit squarely at the back of the ball. Your shoulders, arms, hands and body need to be co-ordinated from the top of the backswing, through impact and on to the finish of the follow through.

At all times during the swing your head should remain steady. If your head moves around throughout your swing you may mis-hit the shot.

When you have a sound swing you can think about hitting the ball harder with your hands because they are in a position to hit the ball hard.

Having a well timed, well co-ordinated swing, with strong arms and hands, will make the ball go a long way. However, if your body timing is not co-ordinated you will only mis-hit the shot.

It is also important to understand the fundamentals which make the ball go a long way. When you swing the club the head obviously moves more quickly than your hands, your hands move more quickly than your body. Your body is the hub. It is like the ice skaters who form a line, half facing one way and half the other, then they skate around in a circle. The skater in the middle is moving very slowly, but those on the outside are going very quickly. In the same way your body moves fairly slowly, your hands move a lot more quickly and the clubhead moves fastest of all because it is on the outside of the arc. It is a fast moving clubhead which will make the ball go a long way, not just a fast moving body. If part of the swing gets out of synchronization you will mis-hit the shot and the ball will not be projected to its full distance.

TIP 93 TEE HIGH TO STOP A SKY

A skied shot is one that is hit with such a descending blow that the ball goes straight up in the air. It is a very destructive shot and although it may have been hit hard, it will not go very far.

Women are prone to hitting skied shots because they tend to tilt in their swings, instead of turning. Women need length more than most men, and so it is even more important to get a square hit at the back of the ball, to get maximum distance.

There are several causes of skied shots. Basically what happens is that the club goes back from the ball very steeply and therefore descends steeply, making the angle of hit very sharp. A sky can be described as a chop; what we are looking for is a sweep.

The first thing to think about is to make sure that you are turning your hips, don't let them slide to the right. Then make sure you turn your shoulders, don't tilt them. Be careful not to lift your arms up in the air as this will cause a choppy action. On the downswing, it is vital that your body turns through the shot.

Often golfers will try teeing their drives lower and lower to stop the ball going so high in the air. This, in fact, will only encourage a steeper swing because you are trying to get the ball up. It is not so much how high you tee the ball which makes it go up in the air, rather the swing path. If you want to stop skying the ball, you need to swing flatter. Try teeing the ball up as high as you can and practise hitting drives. When you tee the ball up three inches

don't ground the club, keep the clubface next to the ball. If when you swing you come under the ball, you know you are still swinging too steeply.

I have a couple of six-inch tees I use for this practice, and I have found it not only useful for stopping a steep swing, but also for promoting a one-piece swing.

TIP 94 DRIVING ON NARROW COURSES

A player who can hit the driver on tight courses really has an advantage over those who cannot. Many players are not confident of hitting the driver when faced with trees on either side of the fairway, and so the long irons are hit, sacrificing length for accuracy.

If you want an advantage on tight courses then you must learn to shape your drives. The most difficult place to aim is right down the middle, especially when you have got trouble on both sides. The one time you need to hit the middle is when there is lots of trouble. By learning to hit a draw and fade with your driver you give yourself more options.

If the fairway is narrow, and slopes from right to left, a shot hit down the middle will finish on the left. A player who can only hit a draw will have to aim at the trees on the right, and may still finish on the left. However if you are able to hit the ball with a fade, the ball will stay in the middle of the fairway.

If you aim at one side of the fairway and shape it back to the middle you are increasing the width of the fairway you have to aim at. Hitting straight down the middle of a fairway forty yards wide only leaves you twenty yards either side. But if the shot is aimed down the right and drawn there is forty yards with which to play.

TIP 95 THE LONG SHOT FROM THE BUNKER

Having the proficiency to play from fairway bunkers is a skill that can save you countless shots.

There are a variety of bunkers that line our fairways, and probably the most feared are tiny pot-hole bunkers. In many cases getting the ball out of these is an achievement. There are also the modern flat bunkers built with course maintenance in mind so that greenkeepers can drive vehicles in to rake them.

These flat bunkers do not hold the same fear for the golfer as do the deep open-mouthed pits that are so common on British links courses.

It is possible to hit long distances from the flatter, shallower sand traps, although this is not normally an option from the deep bunkers.

The key to playing good long bunker shots is in hitting the ball before the sand. If you hit the sand first it will slow the head of the club tremendously and sand will get between the face and ball, causing it to travel only a few yards. It is better to have a complete thin, as long as the ball gets out of the trap, than risk hitting behind the ball and leaving it in the bunker.

With this in mind, your set-up and swing should enable you to play a shot that, even if it goes wrong, will still get the ball going forwards.

The shot you decide to play from the bunker will depend on how the ball is lying, and how close it is to the lip or edge of the bunker.

If the ball is in a good lie, you can go for the green, and even hit a wood if necessary. Place the ball back in your stance, which will promote a 'ball first' hit. Put your hands forward. Hold the club a little more firmly than you would normally to eliminate too much wrist action. Take a three-quarter swing and make sure you hit well through, don't stop at the sand.

You must rely on the swing and not try to help the ball out.

If the lie is not that good then a more lofted club should be hit. You still want to concentrate on hitting the ball first, unless the ball is under the lip, when you should revert to a normal sand shot.

TIP 96 LOW AND SLOW FOR THE LONG IRONS

Many lady golfers have a tendency to use their fairway woods rather than hit a long iron, because they can swing a wood more easily and feel that a bad shot with a wood will go further than a bad shot with an iron.

When they occasionally do attempt to hit the longer irons, they take one look at the straight face of the club with little loft and are not confident of getting the ball airborne. The tendency is to try to help the ball up, hitting a scoop which fails to produce any power and often results in a top or thin.

Even low handicap golfers often have trouble hitting their long irons.

Mastering the long iron can only be achieved with good timing and tempo.

The first thing to remember is that you have one swing and fourteen clubs, not fourteen swings and one club. So when you use the long iron, you want to swing with the same nice easy tempo that you use if you are hitting the 8 iron. If you try to rush the shot your body will become unco-ordinated – either your hips will clear and your hands will be

late, or your shoulders will turn through and leave the rest of your body behind.

When hitting my long irons, I think 'Low and slow'.

If I take the clubhead back with my hands, shoulders and body at the same time, the clubhead will start low to the ground, in a sweeping action. You can only begin to do this when you swing slowly. Keeping your body co-ordinated is vital to the result of shots with longer irons. Throughout the swing an even tempo is vital.

It is important at impact that your hips clear, and that you don't sway forward. With your hips clearing there is lots of room to hit firmly through the shot. Learning to hit firmly down and through will make the ball go up in the air and give you confidence so that, even though the long irons have less loft than your fairway wood, you can still get the ball airborne.

TIP 97 SUCCEEDING IN BAD WEATHER

If you play golf in Great Britain, you must resign yourself to the fact that you are going to play in bad weather.

Furthermore, low handicap players are supposed to perform well despite the conditions. If you say you will not play in the rain, remember that even the 'fair weather golfers' get caught out sometimes.

A well-equipped golfer should never be completely caught out. Umbrella, waterproofs and towels are a must for winter golf; so are a positive attitude, a knowledge of how to cope with the conditions, and a fighting spirit that will not be beaten by the elements.

I can remember an England training weekend at Hoylake one winter. It was freezing cold, blowing a gale, and worst of all I was out playing in the middle of it. Some of the girls gave up and came in, but a few of us battled on, scoring terribly; it was an achievement just finishing. Although I don't think the bad weather practice improved my swing, it taught me that during competition I should keep trying. For one reason or another, many players will give up. They probably won't walk off the course, but in their minds they have given up – the course is too difficult, it's too windy, the greens are ridiculous, it's too cold, there might be a hundred reasons. From this I learnt that whatever the circumstances, I could either give in or I could try making the best of things and try to enjoy doing it. I don't advise giving yourself pneumonia to prove you have staying power, but a certain amount of practice in bad weather is good for your golf.

The first thing that you must en-sure your grips stay as dry as possible. The grips are the link between the body and the club, and if you don't have a firm hold of the club the shot will break down right there. I have cord grips on my clubs. They are very similar to regular grips but with little pieces of cord through them, which gives extra traction, especially in the wet.

It is also vital to have a good set of waterproofs. Make sure that they are long enough to cover your back when bending forward. You may also need warm gloves. My hands are continually cold, and I have found ski gloves made specifically for very cold wet weather are excellent.

When you play with lots of clothes on, waterproofs, thermals, sweaters, etc., it stands to reason that your swing will not be as fluid, your turn not so full. Put to that some rain and wind and it can feel impossible to strike the ball well. Make sure that you don't fall into the trap of hitting the ball too hard because the conditions make the course play longer. Take more club and swing a little shorter. Keeping your tempo in the wind will be difficult, especially if you are tall like me; once again, being determined will help pull you through. I try to put more pressure towards the inside of my feet and keep my legs tighter than usual to prevent movement off the ball if it is very windy.

Lastly, be patient. If you can't get up on a hole because it's into the wind or the fairway is waterlogged, try playing the ball into a position where you can chip and putt. If there is a difficult carry, play safe. Remember, in bad conditions those around you will probably be doing silly things.

FORGET THE LATE HIT

There has been much talk about the advantages of what is called a 'late hit' and much confusion as to what it is and who should try it. The late hit refers to the hands delaying the hit to the ball, whilst the body continues through. The hands then whip in and hit the ball a long way, due to the fact that they hit the ball at the last minute.

Often when golfers study the professionals' swings it looks at impact as though the clubhead is being held back, in a cocked position, by their wrists whilst their bodies are well through the ball.

It is very important to understand that in the golf swing the pace that your body is swinging will affect the pace that your hands should swing. Your body is the centre of the hub and will move more slowly than your hands, your hands are in the middle and will move more slowly than the clubhead. Your tempo is the speed at which you co-ordinate these movements and hit the golf ball. If you try to make a part of your body lag behind it can have disastrous effects.

I sometimes meet ladies who are attempting to apply this late hit theory. Most of them, when trying to hit late, don't hit at all. They either shank the ball, hit it from the heel or hit the shot out right.

Ladies should concentrate more on hitting the ball 'EARLY'. Very few ladies have enough muscular strength to hit down and through the ball as the men do. It is therefore important to build a strong hit another way.

Endeavour to hit the ball early whilst practising. Hit about ten 5 irons normally. Then hit ten shots trying to hit the ball as early in the downswing as your hands will allow. In attempting this you will have to move your body more quickly to time the shot. Moving everything through faster will help hit the ball further only when you can time the shot with your hands.

PLAYING THE COURSE

Away

Playing an unusual course for the first time can often be quite daunting, especially if, like at St Andrews, you have to aim in what seems totally the wrong direction. If you have the opportunity for a practice round, then that will help when you come to play a competition round. But what about those times when you don't get to practise?

When you are faced with what to do on a course that you don't know you must not take any silly chances, you have to play safe and be patient. You must make use of all the information available, yardage charts, direction markers and the like.

At home

It is easy to lose concentration when you play your home course, as we all know how familiarity breeds contempt.

Is there a hole on your course that you always mess up? One hole that, if your card is going to be ruined, will be the troublesome hole? Or maybe a bunker that you can't get out of, and your ball seems to make a bee-line straight for that bunker?

Learning how to cope with problems we encounter on the golf course is one of the strategies in playing the course. I remember, when I first started playing golf I had one such problem. It was the sixteenth hole at Long Ashton. I used to call it my Bermuda Triangle because I always lost a ball there. As a beginner I obviously had fairly weak hands and arms and used to hit a slice. The sixteenth is a dog-leg right, with out of bounds on the right. It's not a long hole, and a good shot down the middle makes it a very simple second shot. However, try as I might, I nearly always hit a ball into the field, out of bounds. Should I have stubbornly continued to hit the ball out of bounds, believing that sooner or later I would hit the fairway, or was there something else I could do. What would you do?

It is my aim to keep this game as simple as possible, and if there is an obstacle that is difficult to get over, I'll try going round. By that I mean, don't limit your thinking to only playing the hole how 'you are supposed to play it' or how the text book or good players play.

If you are a beginner and there is a bunker you can't get out of, then it's better to take three shots going round it than to take a chance of going in it. If there is a tee shot which you keep getting wrong, then take a 4 iron or a 7 iron, even a putter if that's what it takes to keep the ball in play.

Some might say that this is being

defeatist, or being negative. Not true, I say. The game of golf is to get the ball in the hole in the fewest strokes possible. It is not how, but how many. If you save yourself a couple of shots by staying out of trouble whilst others around you are going into it, all the score card will show is a figure. There might be times when people will call chicken, but I believe it will be you who have the last laugh.

TIP 100 — GOLF FOR THE OVER 60S

'I wish I had started playing when I was younger', is the comment I hear more than any other as I go round the country giving clinics for the ladies' section of many clubs.

I started playing golf when I was seventeen, and I wish I had started playing when I was younger. My tip for the over 60s is not to look back, don't worry about what you could have done. It's what you can do now that is important, and *No*, you're not too old to learn and *Yes*, you can play golf at any age.

Golf is obviously more difficult the older you get, any sport is, but that doesn't mean that you can't play. There are certain rules, however.

Firstly, you can't swing as the text book says, unless you are extremely supple. Your muscles will not allow a ninety degree turn with your shoulders and forty-five degree hip turn. You will still need to turn your body, but only go as far as you can comfortably. It is very important that you keep your back straight and bend from the hips; make sure you maintain this plane throughout your swing.

Secondly, don't get clubs that are too heavy for you, they can cause tennis elbow. Make sure you get fitted out by someone who knows what they are doing.

Don't try and do too much too soon. If you find eighteen holes too much, just play nine or five, whatever you feel comfortable with. This doesn't excuse you from building up to play more. If you start on five holes, try six next month and so on.

Accept the fact that you will not be one of the long hitters and aim to make yourself one of the best putters and wedge players. You will not have the strength to become a great striker of the ball, but there is no reason why you shouldn't be a great putter. If you make the most of your short game you will more than compensate for length.

Lastly, golf can be a tremendously exasperating game. Don't worry if you think you are not improving. It might take a little longer than when you were twenty, but you'll still get tremendous enjoyment if you persevere.

Glossary of Golfing Terms

ADDRESS When a player has taken her stance and grounded her club she is said to have 'ADDRESSED THE BALL'

AIR SHOT A swing that did not make contact with the ball when it was attempted

ALBATROSS A score three under par on a hole, i.e. a two on a par five

ALL FLAT The match is level

ALTERNATE A reserve

AMATEUR According to the rules of golf an amateur is someone who plays purely for a non-profit-making motive

APRON The area around the green normally cut shorter than the fairway

ARC The path that the head of the club travels during the swing

ARTISAN Originally called 'working men golfers', they play at certain British Clubs, as a separate part of the club, they have their own club house and have various playing restrictions and pay lower subscriptions

AS IT LIES Refers to the ball. According to the rules of golf you can't move the ball but must play it 'as it lies'

ATTEND Hold, normally referring to the flagstick, which is pulled out of the hole before the partner's ball hits the pin or enters the hole

AWAY The furthest player from the pin has to play and would be told either 'it's your shot' or 'you are away'

BACKDOOR A putt entering the hole from the back as opposed to the front, at which you are aiming

BACK NINE Last nine holes of the course

BACKSPIN Spin put on the ball which makes it stop

BACKSWING The movement of the body taking the club back from the ball

BAFFY Old wooden club similar to a 3 or 4 wood

BALL AT REST Refers to the ball once it has completely stopped moving

BALL MOVED A ball is deemed to have moved if it leaves its original position

BANDIT Slang for someone who plays better golf than their handicap would suggest

BETTER BALL Where two players form a team taking the better score at each hole

BIRDIE One under par, i.e. a two on a par three

BISQUE A stroke given by the lower handicap to the higher, with the advantage that they can use it wherever they choose as opposed to where the stroke index indicates

BLIND HOLE Where the green can't be seen from either the tee or the fairway

BOGEY The old way of scoring on each hole, decided by what a scratch player would have on each hole

BOGEY One over par

BOLD Hit past the hole

BORROW How much the putt moves on a sloping green is how much it 'borrows'

BOUNDARY The perimeter of the golf course

BRASSIE Old-fashioned number 2 wood

BUGGY Slang for an electric vehicle transporting golfer and clubs around the course

BUNKER A hollow filled with sand

CADDIE Person who carries a golfer's clubs

CARD Chart with the par of each hole, the stroke index, often the course layout and space for golfer's score on each hole

CARRY Distance the ball flies in the air

CASUAL WATER Water that is not a hazard and wouldn't normally be there, i.e. a puddle

CHIP A short approach shot

CHOKE Hold down the grip to obtain more control or play a shorter shot

CLEEK Old-fashioned long iron

CLOSED STANCE Aiming right of the ball-to-target line

CLOSED FACE Clubhead aiming left

CLUB Implement used to hit the golf ball

CLUB Venue where golfers meet and play golf

CLUBHEAD The part of the club at the end of the shaft

CONCEDE To give the hole or match to the opponent before it is finished

COURSE Area where play is permitted

CUT Hit a shot from left to right

CUT-UP Shot hit high with backspin

DEAD A ball that finishes so close to the hole that the next shot can't be missed

DIMPLES The small cavities all over the ball

DIVOT Piece of turf which comes from the ground

DOG-LEG Hole which has a bend in it

DORMIE The state in a match when a player is up by as many holes as there are left to play. Dormie 3 means three holes up with three to play

DOUBLE BOGIE Two over the par on a hole

DRAW Match finishing tied between two opponents

DRAW Shot moving from right to left

DRIVE Hit from the tee

DRIVER Number 1 wood

DUCK HOOK Severe shot moving quickly from right to left

DUFF Hit the ground before the ball

DUFFER Slang meaning a not very good player

EAGLE A score of 2 under par on a hole, i.e. a 2 on a par 4

ECLECTIC Competition where the best score for each hole is worked out over several rounds

ETIQUETTE The conduct of a golfer whilst at the course

FACE The part of the bunker facing the golfer

FACE The front of the clubhead

FADE Shot which moves from left to right

FAIRWAY	The mown part of the course between tee and green
FEATHERIE	Old-fashioned golf ball
FLAGSTICK	Thin pole used for marking the position of the hole
FLANGE	Large projecting part on the sole of the sand wedge
FLAT SWING	A lower plain of swing
FLUFF	Hit behind the ball
FOLLOW THROUGH	The part of the swing after impact
FORE	Watch out, ball coming in your direction
FOURSOME	Two golfers playing alternate shots with one ball
FRONT NINE	First nine holes on the golf course
GIMMIE	A friendly way of asking for the putt to be conceded
G.U.R	Ground under repair, a portion of the course marked out where you may lift your ball and drop outside the marked area
GRAIN	Direction in which the grass grows
GREEN	Area of the course used for putting
GREEN FEE	Chare for playing a course
GREENSOME	Two players would play as a regular

	foursome with the exception that both players drive and may choose which shot they play, from then to the completion of play they will play alternate shots
GRIP	The way a golfer holds the club
GRIP	The cover for the end of the shaft which makes it easier to hold the club
GROOVE	The horizontal indentation on the face of the club
GROUNDING THE CLUB	Touching the ground with a club. Not permitted in hazards
GUTTY	Old-fashioned golf ball
HALF	The hole is halved when players have the same score
HANDICAP	Shows the ability of the player and allows for players of different standards to enter the same competition with equal chance of winning
HANGING LIE	Ball lying on a downslope
HAZARD	Bunker or water on the course
HEAD	The part of the club which hits the ball
HICKORY	'Hickory' wood, was used to make shafts before steel and graphite

HIT	A forward blow to the ball
HOLE	4¼ inches in diameter, a ball has to enter it before a hole is complete
HOLE	Part of the course from tee to green
HOLE OUT	Continue to putt until the ball is holed
HOSEL	Neck of the clubhead
IRONS	Clubs made of steel
JUNGLE	Slang for rough
KNOCK OUT	Competition where if you lose you are out
LAG	Normally referring to putts, where a golfer will not go to hole the putt but instead just to get it close
LIE	The position of the ball when it comes to rest
LINE	The direction the ball will travel if it is to go into the hole
LINE UP	Positioning your body so that you will hit the ball towards the target
LINKS	Courses by the sea
LIP	The edge of the hole or bunker
LOFT	The degree of angle on each club
MARKER	Small flat disc used to show the position of the ball on the green when it needs lifting
MASHIE	Old-fashioned 5 iron

MASHIE NIBLICK	Old-fashioned 7 iron	PRACTICE SWING	Trial swing before hitting the ball
MATCH PLAY	Match against opponent where individual score does not count	PREFERRED LIES	Same as placing
		PULL	Shot which goes straight left
MEDAL	Competition where your score on each hole is added up	PUSH	Shot which goes straight right
		PUTT	Shot played with the putter, normally on the green
NET SCORE	Score after the handicap has been removed		
		PUTTER	Club used for putting
OPEN STANCE	Body aiming to the left	ROUGH	Long grass down the sides of the fairways
OPEN CLUBFACE	Clubface aiming right	RUN	Distance the ball travels after landing
PAR	Each hole is given a par depending on how long it is. Par for the course is the total number	SCRATCH	A player who has a handicap of scratch, or 0, should go round the course in par
PENALTY STROKE	A shot added to your score for infringing the rules, hiting into a hazard or losing a ball	SEMI ROUGH	The length of grass between fairway and rough
		SHANK	A ball hit out of the hosel of the club which goes straight right
PIN	Flagstick		
PITCH	A short lob to the green	SHORT GAME	The part of the game played around the green
PITCH MARK	Dent made when the ball hits the putting surface	SLICE	A shot which curves very much from left to right
PLACING	During the winter, or bad weather, you may mark, lift, clean and place your ball, if it is on the fairway	SOLE	Bottom of the club
		SQUARE	Lined up with the target correctly
		STABLEFORD	Competition where you get points for your score on each hole i.e. Bogey 1 point, Par 2, Birdie 3
PLUGGED	Ball which stays in its pitch mark when it lands		
POT BUNKER	Small round bunker		

STANCE	How you stand to hit the ball
STROKE	Action of hitting the ball
STROKE	Another name given to a shot given by a low handicap player to a higher handicap player
STROKE INDEX	Each hole is given a number depending on its difficulty, this is known as the 'stroke index' and it will show where a high handicap player can claim shots from the lower handicap player
STROKE PLAY	Score on each hole added up to give total
SWEETSPOT	Area on the clubface where the ball should be hit
SWING	Backward and forward movement used to hit the golf ball
SWING THOUGHT	A thought which focuses your attention during the round of golf, i.e. 'start back slowly', 'turn my shoulders'
TAKE AWAY	The start of the backswing
TEE	The starting point for each hole
TEE PEGS	Used for teeing up the ball, made of wood or plastic about 3cm long with a point one end and a cup at the other

TEMPO — The pace at which you co-ordinate the swing

THIN — A shot where the bottom edge of the club hits the middle of the ball causing a lower flight than normal

TIMING — All the parts of the swing moving to the impact area at the correct time

TOP — A shot that only hits the very top of the ball

TORQUE — A shaft twists as well as bends during the swing, the torque refers to the twist

TRAJECTORY — The flight of the ball through the air

TRAP — Another name for bunker

WHIPPING — Wax thread used for binding the head of a wood to the shaft. Also referred to as binding.